D0065983

What a

Difference

a Year

Makes

JEREMY P. TARCHER/PENGUIN

a member of

Penguin Group (USA) Inc.

New York

What a
Difference
a Year
Makes

How Life's Unexpected Setbacks
Can Lead to Unexpected Joy

■

BOB GUINEY

Most Tarcher/Penguin books are available at special quantity discounts for bulk purchase for sales promotions, premiums, fund-raising, and educational needs. Special books or book excerpts also can be created to fit specific needs. For details, write Penguin Group (USA) Inc. Special Markets, 375 Hudson Street, New York, NY 10014.

Jeremy P. Tarcher/Penguin
a member of
Penguin Group (USA) Inc.
375 Hudson Street
New York, NY 10014
www.penguin.com

Library of Congress Cataloging-in-Publication Data

Guiney, Bob.
What a difference a year makes : how life's unexpected setbacks
can lead to unexpected joy / by Bob Guiney.
p.   cm.
ISBN 1-58542-301-7
1. Guiney, Bob.   2. Television personalities—United States—Biography.   I. Title.
PN1992.4.G85A3   2003   2003061381
791.45'028'092—dc22
[B]

Printed in the United States of America
1   3   5   7   9   10   8   6   4   2

This book is printed on acid-free paper. ∞

Book design by Meighan Cavanaugh

To my nephew Jack,

so you won't have to make

the same mistakes

I have

ACKNOWLEDGMENTS

There are so many people who I wish to thank for this opportunity. As a young man, "born and raised in South Detroit" (aka Downriver), I always said I would one day write a book. And with thanks to those listed below, and I'm sure some that I forgot to mention, I have a dream come true.

Please understand that it is a given, as I will say it a million times, that I love each and every one of you (albeit in different ways).

With love, thanks, and dedication to: Robert L. Guiney, Ruby B. Sandifer, L.A. "Doc" Sandifer, and L.A. "Andy" Sandifer. As I've said before, please know that wherever you are, as long as our memories are alive, so in our hearts will all of you be.

To my mom and dad, thank you for always believing in me, no matter how ridiculous the ideas that I have had were. You have always supported me, regardless. Thank you for having faith that I will make the right decisions in my life. You are amazing parents and I love you. To Dee Dee and J.D., thank you for being two of my very best friends, and for being two of the "rocks" in my life. You've always been there, without fail, when I've needed you most. I love you both dearly. To Grandma Guiney—thank God I have you, Grandma. Thank you for all of the lessons and memories, and for being such a fixture in our lives.

ACKNOWLEDGMENTS

I realize how fortunate I am to have grown up with you so close, not only in proximity, but also especially in my heart. To Greg and Katina Clausen—thank you for your unfailing friendship, your love, and for the opportunity to pursue all of this by assuming so much of the burden. To Beeba Siaje-Hamieh and Janaya Black, my two faithful and loving assistants, without whom none of this would have ever been possible. I love you both. Thank you for allowing me the opportunity for a second chance. To Amy Hertz and everyone at the Penguin Group: As the infamous "woman on the plane," I have Amy to thank for so much! Thank you for having the vision to realize what I hadn't, and for your show of faith in me by giving me the opportunity to see what could happen if we tried. And to Penguin, thank you for making me feel like part of the family and for working so hard. To Bonnie Solow, my literary agent and trusted sounding board, your warmth and genuine caring for me mean the world to me. I'm so thankful to have you in my corner. Thank you so much. To Elsa Hurley, my collaborator, thank you for taking the time to help me find my voice and for showing me how to put it together so eloquently. You're a truly amazing talent, and I'm so appreciative of what we've done together. To Next Entertainment (Mike, Lisa, Sa, Jason, and everyone else there whom I love), thank you for seeing something in me that broke "the image," and for your love and for believing in me, regardless of the risk. And thanks to you for providing me the opportunity to be who I am and for never questioning me on it. I love all of your asses. To Telepictures and to ABC, thank you so much for giving me a chance and the support to make all of this possible. Thank you for all of it. To Brett Hansen, Marisa Devins, and UTA, thank you for your support of me and for your guidance. I know how well surrounded I have been, and I am grateful. To Ms. Oprah Winfrey, thank you so much for helping to guide me in the right direction, and for being a role model as someone who has never forgotten where she's from and who always remembers to forge ahead. To Jennifer and her family, everything happens for a reason. Had we never loved each other, neither of us would be where we have arrived today. I am so grateful for our past and our future together as friends. Thank you from the bottom of my heart for everything we have shared. To my nephew Jack, I believe in you. Thank you for giving me the inspiration to believe in love again, and for helping me to remember the beauty of a dream. To Dok, Weaz, Kipp, Yam, K. Steele, Looch, Rza, Roach, Chrissy, Casey, Jimmer, Ozzy, Jacko, and everyone who spent the time with me at each of these steps along the way, thank you for being such great people, and even better friends. To my friends from *The Bachelorette* and the women whom I hope to count as friends from *The Bachelor,* thank you for sharing in the two most unique experiences of my life. Arguably, we are all tied to one another for the rest of our lives. To the fellows, I can't thank you enough for your friendship and support throughout all of this. We shared a "once in a lifetime" experience, and I consider all of you to be my friends. To the ladies, although I haven't met you yet, I hope to walk away from this experience with each of you knowing how much I'm sure I will have appreciated the chance to meet you, and that I will be as honest as humanly possible with each and every one of you. My hope is to be able at least to be your friends in the end, as well. To Eric Champnella, thank you for blazing the trail and writing *Olive Juice.* It helped me through some tough times, and I truly appreciate your friendship and your work. To John Tracy and Steve McCornack, thank you for your ability to pass along your wisdom and your willingness to listen when that was all that I needed. You both have affected me tremendously, and I thank you for that.

To all my family and friends, those who are listed on these pages and those who aren't (there are far too many who aren't that I am so thankful

ACKNOWLEDGMENTS

to), please know how grateful I am to you for being there when I really didn't want to get out of bed. Because of the love and support that you all have given to me, I realized the person who I always knew I was . . . but I had just forgotten where I was headed for a minute. You showed me, through you friendship, loyalty, and love for me, exactly which way to go. I'm a better person and a better man as a result of knowing you. I'm indebted to each of you forever. I truly love each of you and wish to express my most sincere gratitude to you for never having lost faith in me. Thank you.

CONTENTS

What a
Difference
a Year
Makes

INTRODUCTION

You probably know me as Bachelor Bob, one of the twenty-five men who vied for the affections of the lovely Trista on ABC's reality TV show *The Bachelorette*. I was the guy who made fat jokes about himself and proclaimed, "Bachelor Bob doesn't dance without music!" before busting out into the Running Man (which America will never let me forget). I had the time of my life, even though I got booted at the end of the third episode.

Maybe you caught me in a clip doing the aforementioned Running Man on the *Late Show with David Letterman* or saw me on *The Wayne Brady Show* or *Live with Regis and Kelly*. Or maybe you saw my weight loss reported what seemed to me constantly on *Entertainment Tonight* and *Extra*. You might have seen me crack Connie Chung up when she asked me how I felt about not being chosen by Trista and I lamented, "Connie, I've cried so many tears, I have none left to cry."

I became popular somehow; I was the everyman, and America responded to that.

One day, ABC was contacted by people from *The Oprah Winfrey Show,* who wanted to have me on. I flew to her set in Chicago, and her hotshot chef taught me how to make Chicken Tagine. I bet that if I had known how to make Chicken Tagine when I was on *The Bachelorette,* Trista never would have given me the ax. Guys, it's the perfect third-date dish to make for your ladies (except you'll never be able to find the necessary "tagine" pot). Oprah's website was inundated with fan mail. And if all that wasn't astonishing enough, I was asked to be the new leading man on the next run of *The Bachelor.* I'll have the chance to meet twenty-five young ladies who have been chosen just for me.

Now, how did that happen? I'm just Bob Guiney, an all-around average guy from Ferndale, Michigan. I'm the neighbor you'd borrow a snowblower from in January, the one you see washing his car in the driveway on summer mornings, the guy who comes out of his house at seven a.m. with his tie loose around his neck and his jacket slung over his shoulder, ready for a day at the office.

I'm like you: I love a summer barbecue with friends; I love playing a pickup basketball game; I love hanging out with friends on the lake and listening to Journey. (Okay, maybe you don't do that.) Most of all, I love my family and friends.

I'm also somebody who's had his heart badly broken. The year before my appearance on *The Bachelorette,* the unimaginable happened—my wife of two years, whom I adored, left me. The pain was so overwhelming that I didn't know how I was going to survive it. Then a recurrence of a bad knee injury sent me spiraling even faster into the trash can.

Somehow, with the help of my family and friends, I managed to claw my way back out. And then—in the most astonishing and improbable turn of events—I went from feeling dumped and unlovable to being America's most unlikely celebrity of sorts. I actually refer to myself as a "pseudo celebrity," but we'll get to that later.

I had gone from my greatest low to my greatest high in the course of one short year. Still, I never thought that anything that had happened to Bob Guiney—mortgage broker, songwriter, and ex–college quarterback—would ever be of such interest to anyone else. But then one day on an airplane, I struck up a conversation with a woman who disagreed. She thought that sharing my experience might inspire others who needed help recovering from a broken heart.

Divorces happen every day, sadly. This is not a book about my divorce, nor is it a story attempting to make me appear as though I'm a sage when it comes to relationships. It is simply an effort to let those who have gone through tough times know that there is light at the end of the tunnel. Especially when there seems to be none.

So here it is—everything I learned during the most difficult year of my life. If what I learned can help you lift yourself up at a time when you might be feeling a little down, nothing would make me happier.

1.

■

FEBRUARY

Sometimes what feels like an end is actually a beginning.
And that's when the real *work starts.*

O N A CRISP winter evening in February, I came home from a weekend trip to Arizona hoping to find my wife. Instead I found a sticky note on the countertop. The message on the note, written in my wife's hand, basically informed me that our marriage was over. I was so upset that I thought the note was signed "J."—not even her full name, was my impression at the time, though I would find out later that I was wrong. That memory of the note struck me as painfully intimate but at the same time shockingly distant.

I had spent the weekend with my buddy Scott Leuchter on a golf course in Scottsdale. I couldn't play much because of a recent "re-twist" of my knee, which was already tender from surgery the previous year, but I had fun riding around in the cart. It was a luxury cart, and it was actually able to pick up some serious speed. As great a time as I was having, I was looking forward to returning home to Jennifer. We had gone through a rough patch in our marriage and had been separated for some time, but we were trying to work things out. I was counting the minutes until we'd be together again, and was hoping that she might have moved back into our house while I was away. I had even bought her a little mesh link bracelet at Tiffany as a surprise gift to try to "bribe" my way back into her heart.

Now there I was, alone: me, the dark kitchen, the empty house, the sticky note. At the time, I couldn't believe that Jennifer hadn't told me face-to-face. As devastating as her news was, the note made it a hundred times worse. Pathetic as it sounds, I suddenly started crying. I ran through the house as fast as humanly possible, calling out Jennifer's name. And when there was no answer, it drove home the reality that she was truly gone.

I composed myself enough to call Jennifer's cell phone. There was no answer, but I kept trying. I must have left twenty messages in the span of an hour. She had left a time for us to talk, but I just couldn't wait that long.

I finally collapsed on the living-room couch where Jennifer and I had snuggled together on Sunday mornings. Now, in Jennifer's place beside me sat the pale blue Tiffany box. I was limp with exhaustion, grief, and shock. I remembered the first time I saw her. I was a senior in college, and she walked into Bennigan's, the bar where I had worked since my sophomore year. I loved that job. I met gorgeous women every day, but when Jennifer walked in, I fell in love on the spot. I had already seen her around, driving a convertible, but I doubted she'd seen me. She had dark hair and porcelain skin and incredible blue eyes. She walked up to me.

"Hi," she said. She blushed slightly—I got the feeling she was shy. "I'm looking for a summer job. Are you hiring?"

"Let me have a word with the boss," I said calmly, and then walked into the back room, where I clutched my hands in front of the manager and begged, "The most beautiful woman just walked in looking for work! You *have* to hire her!"

"Does she have hostessing experience?" he asked.

"Who cares!"

"Is she of age to work in a bar?"

"Yes . . . I don't know. But I think I'm in love."

He sighed, then put a cigarette between his lips, lit up, and inhaled deeply.

"Fine," he said. "Tell her when training starts."

So she was hired. We got to spend a lot of time together, and I was moved by her kindness. She listened patiently to the stories of the old drunks who came early in the afternoon to sit at the bar, and she had a soft spot for my music and poetry. She seemed a little naïve, but also very independent. It's a combination a lot of guys find attractive—you want to take care of her even though you know she can take care of herself.

One weekend we loaded up my Jeep and drove eight hours to western Pennsylvania, where my family owns some land. We had great fun hiking and mountain biking through the foothills, and spent some time with my Uncle Al, who insisted on cooking us burgers on his famous garbage-burning grill. The problem—other than the smell of burning garbage—was that Jennifer was a vegetarian. She rolled with it, though, and showed me that she wasn't just a pretty face—she was a trooper. During that trip, I think we both realized that the relationship had serious potential.

■

WHEN THE APPOINTED hour finally rolled around and Jennifer called back, it was close to midnight. The moment I heard her voice, I realized I loved her more than ever.

"Don't do this," I pleaded into the phone.

"I have to," she said. In her eyes, our marriage was over.

"We can work it out," I begged. "We'll make an appointment with one of the counselors." *One of the counselors*—meaning my therapist or her therapist or the marriage counselor we had seen together. In recent months it seemed as if we had spent more time together in therapists' offices than anywhere else. I had resisted marriage counseling when Jennifer had first suggested it many months earlier (there was something creepy about having a stranger present while you talked about intimate issues with your wife—in my mind, it was like having a Peeping Tom outside your bedroom window while you're making love), but once I started going I realized that therapy could be a good thing. I really thought our young marriage might get stronger because of these sessions.

"There's no point in therapy anymore, Bob," Jennifer said, sighing. "We need to get divorced. Nothing's changed . . . nothing's better."

"C'mon, honey," I said. "We have to find lawyers before anything can happen. I know tons of guys who are attorneys—I sold advertising to them—if it comes to that." It was a bad habit of mine to automatically put the wants of others before my own at the most inopportune moments, almost as if it could buy me some time. Even as I said I'd help her, I knew how ridiculous I sounded—as if I could really go shopping with her for divorce attorneys the way other married couples went looking for blenders. But I would have done anything just to see her, and I thought if I could see her, I could fix it.

"I've already found a lawyer," she said.

Her words knocked the wind out of me. Just a few hours earlier I had been racing along the freeway from the airport, driving well above the speed limit (as usual) because I couldn't wait for the possibility of spending an evening with my wife, and now I felt like I was still speeding, but in a wild, hopeless way, like I was about to go hurtling off a cliff.

She said we had an appointment with the lawyer the next week and gave me directions to the office. "Please, Bob, will you be there?" she asked.

I was so stunned I couldn't form any words. I choked out something that must have sounded like a yes, because she gently thanked me, said she loved me, and then hung up.

Afterward, I just sat in the dark. I wanted so much to reach over and turn on a light so I could see our wedding picture sitting on the mantel, but I was scared that if I did I would discover that Jennifer had taken it down before she left. I wanted to cry, but I felt as if I had squeezed out every last tear. Later, when I saw that the photo was still there, it honestly made me even more sad. In my mind, it meant she didn't want any memories from our wedding.

I don't remember the following week clearly. I must have gone to work, I must have eaten something, but maybe I didn't. The night before the meeting with her attorney, I felt a little more hopeful. I thought that maybe if she saw me again she would change her mind and agree to another try. We had always been such a team. I remembered one night, years earlier, during the height of the grunge era, when we went with our best friend Kevin Donathan ("Dok") to a Pearl Jam concert without any tickets. "We'll get in," I had assured Jennifer. We clung together as we wove through the crowd in the parking lot, looking for scalped tickets. We almost got our asses kicked by some roadies who hated scalpers and their customers.

"I'll find tickets somehow," I told her.

"No, I will," she said, laughing. We loved to outdo each other. She told me to stay put, and then disappeared. Fifteen minutes later, she showed up with Dok and a lanky guy wearing ripped-up jeans and a flannel shirt. Jennifer had met him while standing outside the entrance to the arena.

The guy was Dave Abruzzese, Pearl Jam's drummer at the time. I was completely blown away! I was like, "Hello, Dave."

"You with this beautiful lady?" he said. I nodded, too surprised to speak. "Too bad for me," he said. Then he took us onto the tour bus for tickets and then through the back entrance to great seats, just to the right of the stage. I think about this the way Jon Bon Jovi says he recalls meeting Bruce Springsteen: almost like a religious experience—but not quite!

This memory was Jennifer's memory, too. We had shared a life that I was sure she would remember once we were in the same room together. We had so much history—maybe too much.

But when I arrived at the attorney's office, Jennifer looked up from her chair in the reception area and nodded briefly. Her dark hair was pulled back in a smooth bun, and she was wearing a black suit—a very businesslike outfit, I thought at first, but then I looked down and saw that she was wearing her favorite strappy shoes, which also happened to be my favorite shoes on her, with her perfectly pedicured toenails painted a deep red. She looked more like she was dressed for a night of dancing. I had the irrational thought that she was going to leave the meeting and head straight to the nearest nightclub for happy hour.

I shook hands with her attorney, a middle-aged man with a crumpled shirt. When we walked into his dirty, disorganized office, I saw the divorce papers sitting on his desk, waiting for my signature. I broke down in front of the attorney, who smiled in a gentle but aloof way. He handed me a pen and said to sign on the dotted line, which would instantly put an end to my life with Jennifer. My ex was nothing if not efficient.

I looked at Jennifer through my tears and said, "Do you really, honestly want me to sign this?" When she said yes, I scratched my name wherever I was told to without even really reading the papers. Then I walked out.

We came back to the house after signing the papers, to have an opportunity to talk away from the attorneys, and for me to tie up loose ends. We talked—or really, Jennifer listened.

Finally, I sat at the kitchen counter and started bawling my eyes out. She was kind enough to listen because she had never seen me so sad. I wanted her to cry too, but she was in a completely different place emotionally. She had done her crying already. She expressed that for years she had dealt with the breakdown of our relationship, while I hadn't. She'd had a chance to start making her peace.

"How can we do this? After all the time we've been together?" I wailed. In a babbling way, I took full responsibility for all the problems in our marriage (and she didn't stop me, I might add). I said that our inability to communicate was all my fault, and so was our lack of intimacy. She casually sipped from a glass of water, looking right at me but not really answering. Because I knew her so well, I knew she was feeling the hurt, too. She just wasn't showing it.

■

THE WEEKS AFTER she left were the worst of my life. People say that divorce makes you feel as bad as when a person close to you dies. I agree, but I also have to think that in some cases it can actually be worse. When someone passes away, you don't necessarily feel rejected, and rejection can have the worst sting of all. It goes way beyond just a simple feeling of loss.

I didn't call anyone or see anyone. My friends and family had no idea what was going on with me. I felt like I was living a double life: During the day I would throw myself into work at the mortgage brokerage firm where I was a partner, but when I got home I'd limp into the living room and order Chinese food. And when it arrived, I'd end up weeping all over the kung pao chicken. Anything could make me burst into tears. The Faith Hill song "Cry," when she pleads with someone even to *pretend* that they're feeling sad, could send me into sobbing fits that I thought would split me in two.

I became pathetically nostalgic for the way things used to be— the times you don't realize are good until they're all over, like when I was a musician right after college. I had gotten into the music business the same way I had done so many things in my life—by basically dumbing my way into it. I had been booking acts for parties, and I came to realize that a lot of the bands were pretty bad. In fact, I thought I had more musical talent than some of the guys who were being paid to perform. I had inherited a love for making music from my paternal grandfather, Bob Guiney. We called him "Grumpa" because of his penchant for being a bit grumpy in a hilarious sort of way. He had done virtually everything—from playing pro football before there was even an NFL to entertaining us all with a great sense of humor and a great singing voice. He had been a popular crooner in the Detroit area in the 1930s and 40s, and had been a regular on local radio shows and at social clubs. My Aunt Becky is very musical, too, and has always been a big influence on me. She has fire-engine-red, curly hair and wears heart-shaped glasses. She has a beautiful singing voice and is always playing her guitar. In fact, Grandpa Guiney taught her how to play. I think it's in the genes, because my Aunt Becky's son Andy is also a very talented singer.

At any rate, I decided to join a band, which was called At Zero, and quickly took it over. I was in charge of the business side of things, but I also had a lot of creative input. I wrote all the song lyrics, as I couldn't play a note on any instrument. Writing songs became one of my favorite things to do.

At Zero soon became popular on the bar and frat-party circuit, and I would go touring with the band for weeks at a time. Soon we changed the name of the band to Fat Amy, after one of the band members' girlfriends, who was named Amy and who called everything "phat." Fat Amy became a regional success and my full-time occupation. I was actually able to get by for a good four years as a full-time musician.

Back then, Jennifer and I were not yet married, but we did share a home, and she never complained about my long absences. Her support showed that she wanted to help me achieve my dreams—and every man wants that in a relationship. She never once asked me to leave the band, even though there was very little money in it. I think it was a testament to our relationship that it stood up to that pressure, at least for a while.

Nonetheless, my constant traveling eventually took its toll. Our lives became increasingly more distant. By the time I decided to hang up the band and get a job that would allow me to make more money, we'd been involved for five years, and the cracks were starting to show. Maybe we had spent so much time apart that we didn't know how to be together. I had been the party boy with the band, the ringleader. I was always on, always ready to stir things up. (Picture the way I was on *The Bachelorette,* with the others in the Guys' House, running around, pouring shots for my buddies.) I think Jennifer had hoped that after all her patience, the energy I had spent on the band would be directed toward her and our relationship. But I immediately moved on to my next project— advertising sales (I was actually ranked #2 at one point at a Fortune 500 company) and then, later, starting up a branch of a mortgage brokerage firm. After a full day of work and maybe— albeit infrequently—a trip to the gym, all I wanted to do was sit in front of the television with a cold drink. I was so wiped out that I couldn't even have a decent conversation. I'd basically throw myself into a TV coma. Jennifer would soon give up and go into the bedroom or the lower level of our home. It was odd to realize, one night, that we were watching the same program on television but in different rooms.

Once, I came home to find Jennifer sitting on the living-room floor. A song called "Slow 44" that I had written was playing in the background, and she was crying. I knew at that point that we were in real trouble and that I needed to do something to hold on to her.

I've always said that I am someone who needs to have an epiphany before I make a major decision in my life. In this case, it was caused by the death of my grandmother—my mother's mother, who was one of my very best friends. She was a Southern belle, a beautiful soul, and she had a lovely singing voice as well. Singing has always been a big thing in our family. When she was young she was as gorgeous as a movie star, and she often said that she and Jennifer resembled each other. Gram aged into a plump, elegant older woman with a rosy face and white curls. She always made sure to wear her pearls and high heels when she went out—not to show off, but as a sign of respect for the person she was with. She believed in respecting others. During my time with the band, a lot of the guys I was hanging out with had the right look for rock—which is not always the right look for grandmothers. They had long hair, and some had tattoos, but my grandma treated them with the same courtesy that she did everyone else. In contrast, since I had grown my hair at the time, I started getting some attitude from people, as if they were making judgments about me based on my appearance, like they just assumed I was a loser who was doing drugs (which I wasn't). But she never bought into that kind of thinking.

One year, my mother (who was absolutely best friends with my grandma—they were practically inseparable) was driving my grandma back home from the cottage when Grandma said she wasn't feeling well, and that she was short of breath. My mom, fearful for Grandma's health, convinced her that they should go to the hospital the next day for an angioplasty, just to make sure she was okay.

After the doctors viewed the results of the angioplasty, they told us that she had so much heart blockage that she needed quadruple bypass surgery immediately. We were nervous about the procedure, of course, but also confident that in the end everything would be fine.

Before the surgery, we were all gathered in her hospital room, making her laugh hysterically. I in particular loved to make her laugh by telling the story of the first time I ever saw Jennifer (of course, totally overemphasizing the silly details). I described how one day I was standing by the side of the road, trying to fix a flat tire on my bike. Along came this gorgeous woman in a convertible. She was with a man, and they were toasting with Dom Pérignon, and as they drove past they splashed mud all over me. This detail never failed to crack her up. We all talked and laughed until it was time to leave. It was tough to walk out.

After the bypass surgery, she was upgraded and seemed to be on the road to recovery. Then, one afternoon, on a day that convinced me I had a kind of sixth sense—one that I did not want, mind you—I suddenly decided to go to my mother and dad's house. I don't know why—it was just a strong feeling that I should be there. When I got there, I learned that Grandma had just taken a turn for the worse. We rushed to the hospital, and we were all there with her while she passed away. It was awful. We all loved her so much.

The hardest part was knowing that my mom had lost her best friend. This was not even three years after she had lost her brother, who had died of a heart attack in his sleep, and her father, and my dad's dad—and now her mother. It was devastating. It was awful for all of us, but I think it was hardest on my mom.

Mom spent the first few weeks hardly eating or sleeping—just crying. Trying to be helpful, I swallowed my pain and grief to put on a show of strength that I hoped would give *her* strength. And so I didn't really grieve the loss of Grandma like I should have, even though I had loved her so much and now missed her so badly. This was a mistake that would come back to haunt me years later.

And as for the feeling that I had some kind of sixth sense, it was because I'd had the same experience—feeling the urgent need to pay an unexpected visit—the day my mom's dad passed, and I had also been with my Uncle Big Red the weekend before his death, and then with my Grandpa Guiney the week of his passing. The idea of having this sixth sense bothered me terribly, although when I mentioned it to my parents, they tried to convince me that it wasn't a bad thing and that I should find comfort in it. I later realized that they were right, and it was just an amazing coincidence that I do find remarkably comforting. But both were devastated by the family's losses. It was an impossible time for my family, a time when we were covered by a heavy shroud of sadness.

Grandma's death was not only a tragedy for me, but also a real wake-up call: I realized that life didn't last forever. We had to live for the present. I had first thought about proposing to Jennifer two years into our relationship, but I didn't because I didn't feel stable enough financially. Now I felt there would never be a *perfect* time; I just had to grab the bull by its horns. Even though I knew we had problems—namely, we could have such a hard time communicating with each other—I bought an engagement ring. I hid the diamond ring for a few days, unsure of exactly when to propose.

Then one afternoon, after having a few days off the road with the band, I came home to find Jennifer on the couch, staring sadly out at the balcony. I asked her what was wrong, and she turned to me and said, "Everything is slipping away." She had opened a cutting-edge clothing boutique and was realizing that it was no longer her passion. It wasn't doing as well as she would have hoped. (Apparently, at the time, East Lansing, Michigan, women were too practical for cosmopolitan styles like clingy off-the-shoulder blouses. It was all about The Gap and college-style apparel.) Jennifer always had such an excellent sense of fashion. Unfortunately, the women of East Lansing were not quite as into fashion at the time. In addition, I was on the road constantly, and she wasn't happy in the town where we lived. It was time for a move—both geographically and in our relationship.

"I'll never slip away," I told her. I pulled out the ring and took her hand. She trembled as I put the ring on her finger. She couldn't speak, but I knew by the way she clutched the ring to her chest that she would marry me. We held each other in silence and wept.

To this day, people who were there comment that our wedding was the prettiest they have ever been to. It was held on a golf course. We set up a tent and put down hardwood floors and had the band play dance songs from every era so that everybody— young and old—would enjoy the music. Jennifer was lovely in a simple, vintage-looking gown. What made her the most beautiful, though, were the tears of joy that shone in her beautiful blue eyes throughout the whole day. After the toast, I rendered her speechless when I got up on the stage and sang Elvis's "Love Me Tender" to her. I had, strangely, never before sung a love song directly to her. It was long overdue.

The question I kept asking myself in the days after she left me was: How did I get to this point? How did I get from the day of our wedding—with both of us so happy and our families and friends there as witnesses to our love—to now, this February night barely

two and a half years later, when I was injured, divorced, and completely alone? I thought about that time I came home to find Jennifer in tears while listening to my song. I hadn't understood the
reason for those tears until a week after she left me for good,
when in a state of despair I riffled through my CDs. I popped them
into the stereo and listened to them in the dark.

One song, "Slow 44," has the lyrics, *We're still standing around in*
squares, wondering who's to blame / for all the years / gone by much quicker
when you're young . . .

I wish I had understood what I was really feeling when I wrote
those words. (I guess that's part of how we try to get though major disasters—by avoiding what's too painful even when it's right
in front of us. It's a healthy denial that becomes a kind of self-
protection.) The song was all about the strain of a relationship
when you're young and trying to make your way in the world.
That's exactly what I was doing—taking steps toward success, and
in doing so I was leaving Jennifer and the feelings of doubt she was
having about our relationship behind. Another line in the song is,
You're still standing around, feeling proud with your Daddy's name. She
never changed her last name after we were married, and in a lot of
ways it hurt my feelings.

I like to think of myself as a modern Renaissance man. For example, my brother-in-law J.D. and I always would laugh and say
that we'd love it if our wives made more money than we did, and
he always said he'd love to be a househusband. I loved his attitude,
but strangely when it came to the whole last-name issue, I was
much more traditional. This again shows the disaster that was my
thought process.

Jennifer explained that she had established herself as an individual—this was her name—and that changing it would mean having to seemingly erase who she had been and reestablish herself. I understood the logic of that, but I always took it to mean (rightly or wrongly) that she didn't want to be part of my family. At first I had been cool with it, but when things started to get bad, it meant more to me. Looking back, I'm not sure exactly what I thought a name change was going to solve, but it came to symbolize a lot.

■

I GREW UP in a very close-knit family, where we were all one another's best friends, and honestly still are. That means I have always had a lot of people watching out for me. With us, it was always family first. Other people were first-and-a-half.

Once, when I was about eight, my cousin was having a birthday. But some kids in the neighborhood were playing kick the can, and I wanted to join them.

"Family first, Bobby," my mother said when I asked if I could join the game, as she cupped my face in her soft hands. And after we'd eaten birthday cake and I'd played a game of "push someone who's dancing on the coffee table to the ground" with my sister, I realized I'd had a better time with my family than I would have had with the neighborhood kids.

My mom taught us that your family will always know you for who you really are—not for the persona you may decide to present to the rest of the world—and because of that, your family can keep you honest in a way that others can't. We've all taken that lesson to heart. It was a family credo of sorts, and still is today. We keep one another very grounded.

The town that my sister, Dee Dee, and I grew up in was called

Riverview, but we get grief from others at times about the name because it's actually the only town in the area *without* a view of the Detroit River. The area where I was raised is called the Downriver
area, and it's a very blue-collar, working-class, former-steel-mill kind
of place. When I went off to college, I found that some of the people
who come from the more upscale areas look down on it, but I have
always taken an enormous amount of pride in being from the Downriver area. I've often thought that Steve Perry wrote the song "Don't
Stop Believin'" about being *born and raised in South Detroit* all about
me. Some of the very best people that I have ever known I met while
growing up there. And many are still my best friends today.

My parents were both raised in Riverview. My mom, Nora, was
the coach for my sister's high school cheerleading team, who were
national champions. My father, whom I'm named after, was a policeman in Riverview for thirty-eight years. He was also a school
board member, assistant baseball coach, and a Boy Scout leader.
He's always been the guy who has done the morally right thing.
For example, once when I was a kid, I walked out of a Majik Mar-
ket with a pack of Juicy Fruit that I hadn't paid for. When my dad
found out, he marched me back to the store and made me pay for
the gum and apologize to the store clerk (who laughed at me). On
the drive home, he talked about how the difference between being
a good person and being a bad person is all in the decisions we
make. I got the message loud and clear at an early age.

I've tried hard to develop the same type of integrity. My friend
Jeff Kipp, who was an Army Ranger, once paid me the biggest
compliment I think I've ever received. He said he thought I'd be a
good Ranger, because I always try to do the right thing, even when
no one's looking. This made me think of my dad. I was especially

moved because I know that Army Rangers know a lot about relia-bility—they have peoples' lives in their hands with every move. So for him to give me this compliment meant a lot to me. And I knew how serious he was in his commitment to being a Ranger, and it made his compliment mean that much more.

I've learned the most about life from my parents, both in what I want to do with my life and what I don't. My mom and dad taught me to care about other people. If someone needed a little help, they'd open their doors and hearts, and they never looked for anything in return. My buddy Scott (the one I visited in Scotts-dale that fateful weekend Jennifer left me) joined my family when we were in the tenth grade because his family was having serious problems. When we were sixteen he moved in with us, and he pretty much stayed with us for the rest of high school. He consid-ers us to be part of his family, and we feel the same. At his up-coming wedding I'll be his best man, and my dad will stand up with him at the altar. It's an enormous honor.

My parents were very giving of their time to their children, and to our friends. We were always the kids that had everyone over—and they all loved our folks. It was great. In high school, my friend André Gaines, or "Silky G," as he called himself, moved in and lived with us when his mother fell ill. He stayed with us for a short time and was literally part of the family from that point forward. This was illustrated about a year later when he was pulled over for speeding and actually challenged the policeman by asking him, "Do you know who my father is?" The cop obviously had no idea, so when André said, "He's Lieutenant Guiney," the cop called in to my father and asked, "Do you have an African-American son named André?" My dad replied that he did and asked the policeman to let

Silky G go on his way, and so the cop let him go with a warning. That's just my parents for you.

When I was growing up, my dad's parents lived next door to us, and my mom's parents lived two streets away. Mom's sister and brothers raised their families in nearby communities. Dad's sister actually lived on the same street, and she had nine kids. Holidays and celebrations were very crazy, crowded events, during which we would tease one another, laugh raucously, eat off one another's plates, and all have just a little too much to drink. It was so nice to have such close-knit family nearby.

As I sat home alone those February evenings, I remembered family gatherings when I think Jennifer went into sensory overload. She'd grab a magazine or book and slip off to another room and read, just for a moment of peace and quiet. She was a gentler soul than any of us were. I think some members of my family wanted her to be as boisterous as we all were, and maybe they felt she was making a statement—possibly saying that she didn't want to be a part of us. And that led to some friction.

I realized that one of the mistakes I made was that I had been too closed off emotionally. I wouldn't talk about things that were bothering me—sometimes I would blame her, wishing she would make more of an effort to get along with my family, and she felt she was trying very hard. I felt that I was trying to keep everyone happy, but she couldn't be bothered. I was always too gun-shy to bring up these issues, because I didn't want to cause a fight. It was such a weak approach; it made me unavailable to her. Then she resented me, and I resented her for resenting me. Can you say "vicious cycle"?

It was soon clear that getting married hadn't solved our problems—it had actually made them worse. Resentment causes barriers, and barriers get in the way of intimacy. Then, because there is no intimacy, there is more resentment. When you never talk about your problems, after a while you forget what they are, and then you have no chance of solving them. I read something in my friend Eric Champnella's book *Olive Juice* that made total sense to me: "We shoved so much stuff under the rug that by the end, we couldn't see each other from across the room."

The situation got so tense that at times, when we were going to be physically intimate with each other, something would happen and the moment would be lost. There's nothing sadder than watching your wife, unbelievably beautiful and very sexy but completely untouchable on the other side of the bed, neither of us wanting to say a word because it would mean admitting that the moment was over.

I've heard it said that when things are good between a man and a woman, the issue of physical intimacy is ten percent of the relationship, but when things are bad, it's ninety-five percent of it. And it's so true. Because Jennifer and I were hardly being intimate, we were left with only five percent of a marriage, and nobody can make anything meaningful out of that.

Somehow we had gone from being two people who couldn't get enough of each other in the beginning to being two people who didn't even know how to touch each other. Combine a lack of intimacy on *any* level with the way we couldn't connect on so many other issues, and what you have is a recipe for disaster.

My college football coach used to say, "If you're not getting better, you're getting worse." Of course he was talking about football, but I think it's true in all parts of life, and it was especially true after my marriage fell apart.

When I was in high school I was the class president and the captain of the football team. In my mind, those accomplishments really defined who I was as a person. Then I got to college and made the team as a quarterback, and I thought, *Well, I've made it. I have arrived.* What I didn't realize was that all the *real* work was just about to begin.

When something good happens, sometimes people have a tendency just to coast. But I don't think you should achieve a goal and say, "Okay, now I've made it. I can just hang out and enjoy." You have to build on that success and go further.

When something bad happens, I think there's even more of a tendency to stagnate. You just close up shop and drift. It's the mistake I made following my divorce.

After several weeks of avoiding my pain by spending too much time feeling sorry for myself and even more time at the office, I tried to begin to face the music. My life had been on a downward spiral for some time, and I realized that getting through the grief and pain was going to be a hell of a challenge.

2.

◻

MARCH

Judge a man by how he behaves when he is at his lowest point,
not by how he behaves when everything is going great.

I N ADDITION TO being sad and lonely, by March I had gained a lot of weight—as if I wasn't already feeling bad enough about myself. Reinjuring my knee meant that I couldn't use physical activity for stress relief—at a time when I needed it most. I'd always played sports—I loved the challenge and the competition and the thrill of victory. I had never really had a weight problem before. The irony of my appearance on *The Bachelorette* was that everyone assumed I'd been out of shape all my life, whereas that was just a brief window of being "bloated." During this time I finally understood what my buddy Dave Rzepecki meant when he said, "Judge a man by how he behaves when he is at his lowest point, not by how he behaves when everything is going great." Life was testing me in a way that I had never been tested before.

Although my world was continuing to fall apart, I still didn't want to tell too many people that I was going through a divorce. I couldn't even tell my parents the details of what I was going through. I only told them that things weren't good. I think they were feeling awful for me, and that bothered me, too. I don't know if I was doing this out of embarrassment or something else. I felt that I needed to muscle through it alone. The only person I tried to talk to was Jennifer, and that didn't help at all. She'd had plenty of time alone to think her decision through, and she had moved on in a way that I wouldn't for several more months. But I would call her anyway, just to hear her voice.

When we're in pain, it's human nature to try to find a way to numb the feeling. Some do it by eating too much, drinking too much, or sleeping too much. That March, I did it by working too much (which I think is the healthiest way to go, given the other options). I'd leave work at eight at night and grab dinner on the way home. Within an hour I'd be in my pajamas, getting sleepy in front of the TV. By six-thirty the next morning, I would be back at the office. My thinking was that if I couldn't have a successful marriage, at least I could have a successful business. My partner, Greg Clausen, had been working in the mortgage industry for years and had tons of contacts, but I didn't because I was so new. So I took that time to really work up to his level.

I was only in the mortgage industry because of Greg. Way back when, he had been working for the same mortgage company for nine years and was miserable. He was doing well for himself, but he still wasn't being properly compensated for the work he did, even though he was the company's top most successful broker. In the meantime, I had been doing very well in advertising sales and had managed to save up some money. But I wanted to own a company, or at least a branch of one, from which I could get residual income. So I started working on him constantly.

"Let's start a mortgage company; let's start a mortgage company," I badgered him endlessly. I said, "I'll get us the dough, and you bring the knowledge and the experience." Greg always thought I was the best salesperson he knew and that I would bring a lot to the business, and he suspected that teaming up might work out brilliantly. Eventually, he was willing to do it, so we started working together, hoping to make a go of it. And then we did.

It was great to have the security of knowing that I could support myself financially. I had started out without a salary and with no guarantees about the future. But now we were hiring people to work for us, and the business was steadily growing. I was also finding that I genuinely enjoyed my work. When I went into it, I'd never written a mortgage before, so I didn't even know if I'd like doing it. But what I found is that although working in the financial industry can sometimes be dry, it can also be very rewarding. I have always looked for a spiritual aspect to the work I do, and I found that I felt good when I was able to help people stop a foreclosure on their home or find money to send a child to college, or to help them out in some other way.

Sometimes I would be so busy that I would almost forget that the love of my life had left me. I wouldn't recommend it for everyone, but in my case overworking was one of the activities that kept me from losing my mind.

As has happened so often with me, the unexpected (and unwanted) changes in my life served as a wake-up call. They caused me to reassess what I was doing and where I was going. In early March, I called my therapist, John, and made an appointment.

MARCH

I have to thank Jennifer for having pushed me to seek counseling in the first place. Several months before she moved out, Jennifer asked me if I would see a marriage counselor with her, but I said I didn't want to. So she decided that if we couldn't go as a couple, she'd go alone. I didn't even know she was in therapy until months later—which just shows how badly communication had broken down between us. When I finally found out she was going, I realized how serious the situation was, and I finally agreed to give counseling a shot.

Ironically, despite how much I'd resisted it, I actually felt a kinship with my counselor almost right away. John was a slender fellow with pale skin and a blond beard. He reminded me a little of my band's guitar player Kirk, because he was so calm and even-keeled. I felt that he was someone who genuinely wanted to help me clearly see things about myself.

Once I'd gotten used to being in counseling and he'd gotten familiar with me and my situation, Jennifer and I went to see him together. I took a lot of the blame in our first session together. John was always sensitive, but he asked the hard questions—the hardest of which was simply, "Why?"

"Why didn't you open up to Jennifer about what was bothering you?"

"Because I couldn't."

"Why couldn't you?"

"Just because. I couldn't."

"Why?" When I didn't answer, he said it was okay just to be quiet. He said I should look inside myself and think. After a moment, I hit a realization.

"I couldn't open up to Jennifer about our problems, because to name something would mean it actually existed. I thought that if I pretended our relationship was perfect, it would be."

John smiled. "But it isn't perfect, is it?"

"Hell, no," I said. "It's almost the opposite of perfect." With that admission, I felt as though a boulder had been lifted off my chest.

Since that meeting had gone well, we decided to take the next step and see someone who specialized in couples counseling. That session was a train wreck. It was during that meeting that I realized she wasn't willing to do anything else to help pick up the pieces. It was really hard to see, because I was still trying to salvage something. At the same time, we were each being as open and honest as we could be. I think even the marriage counselor could see how much she still loved me and how much I loved her.

When I got to John's office for our next appointment after the disastrous couples session, I plopped down on his couch and exclaimed, "Get ready for an earful." Then the dam broke. I told him how I still loved her and how much I still wanted to make the marriage work, and how devastating it was that she didn't seem to want to try anymore. He nodded his head in encouragement but never interrupted me. When tears came spilling out of my eyes, he leaned over and handed me the box of tissues he kept on the table beside him.

After he was sure I was finished, he said something that has stuck with me to this day: "Do you really want to be with someone who doesn't want to be with you anymore?"

I have come to think that everybody has to ask this question when trying to deal with a failed relationship—whether it's a marriage, a friendship, or even a business partnership. If someone has changed their mind about you—that person no longer laughs at your jokes, no longer likes to hear you sing, is no longer interested in hearing about your day—you should probably take it as a sign that you should be reevaluating your commitment to that relationship and to that person.

"Bob, I saw almost right away that you have a tendency to beat yourself up," John told me. He leaned back in his chair and pressed his hands together. "I think you take the blame for everything, without taking the time to figure out whether or not it's actually anyone's fault."

"But it's easier just to take the blame than to blame the person you love, especially when at times you agree with everything they're upset about," I protested.

"It may be easier, but it's not always the truth, and until you understand the truth about a difficult situation, you're not going to be able to solve it." He cleared his throat. "You know, Bob, in every divorce, there are always three sides to a story—your side, the other person's side, and the truth. And at the root of that truth is that it's never all one person's fault, whether or not he or she is willing to take the blame."

I didn't respond, but I felt a flood of relief at his words. For weeks, I had been claiming responsibility, and this was the first time someone had suggested that maybe it wasn't entirely my fault after all.

"There are a lot of things in a relationship that people just can't control," he continued. "If they could control everything, we therapists would be out of a job." John gave me a sad smile. "You could be the greatest person on Earth, but that doesn't mean you'll have a happy marriage if you're married to the wrong person, no matter how great the other person is."

This reminded me of what Jennifer had said to me one day after our divorce. She said, "You can have two great people, but that doesn't mean that they're supposed to be married." She was right.

I sat back and closed my eyes. I truly didn't know how things could have gone so terribly awry. I thought about the November before the sticky-note incident. I had come home after Thanksgiving and met up with her at the christening of my soon-to-be-godson Connor. Two of our best friends, Gregg and Melanie, had asked me to be the godfather to their firstborn son. I couldn't have been prouder. Things hadn't been great with Jennifer and me, but I guess I hadn't seen just how "not great" they had become.

Jennifer told me that day that she felt it would be best if we separated for a while to figure out where things were going. She thought that maybe some distance would help us solve our marriage problems. The timing of the announcement was pretty rough, but I realized I had let things slip a bit too far to make any call at that point. She informed me that she and I would see each other once a week, with the thought that if we started dating each other again, we would recapture those initial feelings from the time when we first fell in love. But it didn't work. In fact, the distance made things worse.

The problem with a husband and wife having scheduled visits is that they can't just pick up emotionally where they left off. At least I couldn't. Instead, they have to start over from scratch every time they see each other, and that makes things too tough.

We both saw that the gap in our marriage was yawning ever wider, and in an attempt to close the distance, we decided to spend New Year's Eve together. The night turned out to be a disaster. We went to a restaurant for dinner, and we ran into a man whom Jennifer had met one night when she was out with her friends. He wasn't a particularly attractive guy by any means, but he was nice enough. He was pudgy and sad, the type of guy Jennifer would be especially nice to because she felt sorry for him—ironically, the type of guy I felt I was becoming, a realization that drove me to the gym yet again.

Still, though, he was one of the primary reasons that I knew we had issues not too many months before. That night when she was with her friends, he got ahold of her cell phone number and called her that same night well past two A.M.

"Who was that?" I asked.

"Oh, that was this guy I met. He's harmless," she said.

I was pissed. I pressed her even more. "What the hell did he want?"

"Don't get jealous," she said. "He's just a friend. I'm allowed to have friends, aren't I?"

"Of course," I responded. "I have no problem with you having guy friends, and you know I trust you completely. I just don't trust him."

She didn't reply, but I added, "And I don't really want guys calling you on your cell so late. Or at all, for that matter."

"Fine," she said with a yawn.

"Fine," I replied, with a feeling that nothing I said mattered at that point.

At the restaurant, I followed her as she went over to say hello. He looked up as she approached and was so startled that he knocked over his water glass. He tried to mop up the water with his dinner napkin as he stammered out an introduction between Jennifer and his girlfriend, who was watching the scene with narrowed eyes. Seeing some guy come undone over my wife was a moment I certainly could have done without, and I don't think Jennifer was too comfortable with the situation, either. After we'd walked away, she said to me under her breath, "Well, maybe you were right about him after all. He's never acted quite like that."

Then we went to a big party at Greg's house. It quickly became clear that this was another mistake. All our friends were there, and they were obviously surprised to see that we had arrived together. Their greetings seemed awkward and forced, and later I saw a couple of them looking our way and whispering.

Jennifer disappeared for an hour—I guess she just didn't want to be a part of the party with me. Later I found out from a friend that she was upstairs in a bedroom, talking in a whisper on the phone to someone—I have no idea who. To be honest, by that point I didn't even want to know—it had all gotten so difficult that I just couldn't take any more bad news. A few minutes before midnight, I was running around like a chicken with its head cut off, trying to find her because I wanted to have the symbolic New Year's Eve kiss, whether or not we actually were going to be ringing in the new year together.

I was running around, pleading with everyone, "Have you seen Jennifer? Jennifer. You know, my wife, Jennifer." I was a complete idiot, although I didn't realize it until much later. She ended up appearing at about fifteen seconds before midnight. As you can imagine, it was a pretty anticlimactic kiss.

I guess neither of us could expect much more of anything physical once we got home—new year or not. Things had slipped so far that we didn't even know how to approach each other anymore.

We kept going to see our separate counselors, and surprisingly, things seemed to take a turn for the better. Maybe she saw that I was finally acknowledging problems and trying to open up in a way that I hadn't in years. We both craved more opportunities to interact.

So Jennifer started staying over more often. We were both trying. Once again, her gym bag sat at the foot of the steps by the front door, and the smell of her perfume permeated the sheets. I loved the smell of her perfume. It was always so sweet and soothing, but never overwhelming—just like Jennifer herself.

There were still long stretches of silence between us—a silence that sometimes felt harder to penetrate than a brick wall. Still, I felt we were on the right track. I felt confident that we would work things out.

One day, I was rushing to work when I slipped and twisted my knee, reinjuring damage I'd done almost a year before when I'd taken a swing out on the golf course. I felt something in my knee snap like a rubber band. Now I had caused the pain to flare up again from that old injury.

At around that time, my friend Scott called and invited me to Scottsdale. With the pain I was in from my knee, as well as the friction we were having at home, I thought a change of scene might be just what I needed. It would also give Jennifer a little alone time, which I thought she could probably use. So I went away for the weekend.

When I got back, I found the sticky note.

Sitting in John's office, everything seemed so random; I couldn't make sense of any of it, and I told John so.

"Real life is something we may never make sense of," John said. "What's important is that we keep moving on."

But at the time I didn't want to move on. If it had been up to me, Jennifer and I would have stayed married forever. We would have been deeply miserable but together. I wanted to do this noble thing for all the wrong reasons—mostly, I think, to keep up appearances, but also just to be with her, even if things were bad.

I left John's office exhausted and confused, but also determined— it would take a lot of work to make peace with what had happened between Jennifer and me, but, by God, I was going to do it.

"I know you'll get through this rough patch," my sister Dee Dee told me over the phone that night. "You're tough."

"Yeah, I guess." She didn't know the worst of it, but just hearing her statement of confidence was a help.

"Hey, did you see that new TV show called *The Bachelor?*" she asked, switching topics suddenly, as she often does.

"No, I didn't catch it."

"Chrissy and I watched it. It was a lot of fun." She said that she and Chrissy were thinking of single women they knew that should apply for the next show. "And we also think they should do a show where a woman gets to pick from a lineup of guys," she added. "You know, just for the sake of fairness."

I laughed. "What, you mean like *The Bachelorette?*"

"Yeah. Maybe we should call ABC and sell them our idea. Hey, you'd be great for a show like that. Except you couldn't go because, technically, you're still married."

That was the perfect opening to let her know about the finality of the divorce, but I still wasn't ready. Instead I asked, "How's my favorite nephew?"

■

SOMEHOW I GOT through March in one piece. My saving grace was my sense of optimism, which I've had my whole life. My mother and my grandmother were unfailing optimists every day of their lives, and they passed that quality on to me. My dad and mom honestly believed that both my sister and I could do anything we wanted if we set our minds to it. This is the kind of support network that had me water-skiing the summer before reconstructive knee surgery (against their better judgment), because I knew I could do it. And I did.

I never think I'm out of the game, even when I'm really out. My dream was to play quarterback in college. My Uncle Big Red had played at Michigan State, and I wanted to follow in his footsteps. A string of injuries and a growing disinterest in the game kept me from ever starting as quarterback in college, even though I was recruited for the position in high school. But I did retain one thing from those days of playing quarterback: No matter what the score is, I think I can still pull it out somehow. I'm a real fourth-quarter quarterback—the John Elway of life's tough knocks. Captain Comeback. The underdog who surprises everybody by winning in the end—despite all the odds.

3.

◼

APRIL

Love your family, because when things go wrong they may be
the only people who are there for you.

GRANDMA SANDIFER

O NE DAY IN April, I came home after work and kicked back with a bento box of fresh sushi I had picked up at a Japanese restaurant. I turned on the television and started flipping through the channels. I stopped when I saw a man in a suit standing next to one of the nicest ocean views I'd ever seen. I left it on while I poured out soy sauce. As I chowed down on spicy tuna, I listened to the host talk about a guy named Alex who had been a swimming star and class valedictorian in high school. That sounded a lot like me, although my sport had been football. He was a successful, hardworking professional—again like me, although I was from the Midwest and he lived on the West Coast. I was watching the reality show *The Bachelor* that my sister had talked about.

The similarities between me and this guy abruptly ended. He

was in great physical shape, proclaiming he was ready to pop the question to Miss Right, whereas I had a reinjured knee and wasn't sure I'd be able to open my heart to someone ever again.

I changed the channel. *Back to the Future* was playing, and I got up and poured myself a glass of lemonade. But after a few minutes of watching Michael J. Fox trying to race his DeLorean past the clock tower at the perfect moment, I found myself picking up the remote and turning back to ABC—the similarities between Alex's life and mine had piqued my curiosity.

I started to feel a little self-conscious as I watched Alex spending time with the young women, trying to get to know them better. I'm a guy—I like watching sports and comedies, not reality dating shows. Nevertheless, I turned up the volume and put my feet on the coffee table. As someone who had recently been dumped, I was oddly compelled by the drama of the fact that this guy had already rejected more than two dozen lovely ladies.

I was fascinated by the spectacle, and I wondered how he knew who to choose based only on the very limited conversations he had with each of them. Personally, I liked Shannon (the prim, auburn-haired accountant) and Trista (the petite blonde who worked as a pediatric physical therapist). They seemed great for him. I thought that overall, Alex made good choices. Once I realized how the show worked, I kept wondering how he was able to remember all their names during the invitation ceremony (which was later called the "rose ceremony") when he'd just met them—especially in the beginning, when there had been twenty-five of them. (I found out later, when I was on *The Bachelorette,* that when Trista was in the deliberation room, she studied our photographs extensively to match names to faces.)

I felt a little foolish after that episode of *The Bachelor* was over. I turned to the local news and didn't plan to watch the show again.

The next morning at work, when I went to the office's kitchenette, Greg was chatting with a few officemates. I hesitated at the door. It was not unusual for us to talk and touch base before starting the workday, but these days I was nervous about getting into a conversation with anyone because I didn't want to reveal what was going on in my personal life. I grabbed myself a bottle of water.

"What did you do last night?" Greg asked me.

"I saw the strangest thing on television. Get this: A guy like us—I mean, *really* just like us—gets to live in a huge house on the beach in LA and date twenty-five women on national television. Can you believe it?"

"Oh, you've finally discovered *The Bachelor*? Where have you been while the rest of the world has been watching it? You have definitely been spending too much time at the office." We laughed and chatted about the show for a couple minutes.

"I'm gunning for Shannon, myself," I said. And then I left. The issue of what was going on in my personal life had been safely avoided.

But it couldn't be avoided forever—word was bound to get out. And it did. This made the first few weeks of April particularly trying for me. By this time, most of my friends and all my family had heard from either me or through the grapevine that Jennifer and I were finished. In fact, the actual date for our divorce to be final was rapidly approaching, and I was clinging to whatever I could to maintain my dignity and composure. Slowly, I was realizing (it was taking me some time to get to the "reality" of this one) that despite the fact that I thought of myself as Captain Comeback, even I might not be able to pull this one off.

APRIL

Anyway, with our "official divorce day" quickly approaching, I spent most of my time just struggling to make it from one day to the next. I made so many visits to John that month, I must have paid his children's way through college.

He helped me see that I had made the same mistake that many young people do—I tried to factor Jennifer into my existing family instead of creating an entirely new family with her as I should have.

Jennifer's relationship with her family was not quite as crazy as mine—but, for that matter, most people's aren't. For one thing, my family discusses everything to death. And I think she was intimidated by how over-the-top and loud my family was.

I remember times when we would be with my family and the tension would be more than a bit noticeable. There was one moment in particular when my mom, who was a smoker at the time, had decided to light up a cigarette in the family room where we were all sitting. Jennifer began waving her hand in front of her face to disperse the smoke, and I immediately jumped up to open the sliding door to bring in some fresh air. The smoke honestly didn't bother me, but the room quickly became tense.

It was awful. Jennifer left the room, while I sat there, trying to figure out how to run interference between them. There were a lot of truly tender exchanges between them over the years, but at the height of our problems as a couple, it honestly seemed like "the tension felt around the world" was between the two of them.

I believe my mother and Jennifer liked each other, but sometimes I felt that neither was ever totally supportive of my relationship with the other, especially in the beginning. I don't know why—maybe they felt threatened or something. Whatever the reason, I know that Jennifer and Mom both picked up on it, and there was friction. And in the end, it may have been something of a mother's intuition to protect her child in a situation that was not right. With Jennifer, perhaps it was a woman's intuition telling her that she was ready to leave, even before she admitted it to herself. I'm not sure.

Generally speaking, I spent the majority of summers balancing the demands and time requests of two families who both loved spending time together—and who both had homes on lakes. It was always difficult to leave one place in the middle of a summer party weekend to cruise to the other family's location. We loved seeing everyone, but meeting the demands was exhausting.

During my marriage I tried to treat the three women in my life—my wife, my sister, and my mother—all equally. But maybe I should have raised my wife above the other two. I don't know. I don't know what the right answer is. Obviously, I'm not trying to pass myself off as a relationship guru . . . just a guy who learned from his own experiences. Take it as you will.

As the date loomed, I felt the need to sit down and talk to my family about the breakup. I suppose I was feeling—rightly or wrongly—a little resentful of them. Maybe if they had made more of an effort to relate to Jennifer, she and I would still be together. It was nuts! But no matter how hurt I felt about their inability to connect with Jennifer at times, the fact was that my family has always been there for me. Keeping the divorce on the down-low had become a problem in and of itself. I hadn't been candid with them when things started to get really bad between Jennifer and me, because I wanted to pretend everything was okay. It was a dumb move—they couldn't offer me help if they didn't even know I needed it. I was concerned that if I told them exactly what was going on, and then somehow she and I worked things out, they would hold it against her. It was stupid logic on my part.

Right after the sticky-note debacle, I remember telling John at one session that I missed my family and wanted to confide in them.

"What's stopping you?" he asked.

"They would want to give me advice, and I don't want it." I knew that my family would never be impartial—they loved me, and it was their job to take my side over anyone else's, so I didn't believe their assessment of my situation could ever be accurate.

"So tell them you don't want advice," John said. "But make sure you clearly communicate everything that you *do* want."

First, I had called my sister, Dee Dee, who's one of my very best friends and confidantes. We haven't always been as close, though. She's three and a half years older than I am, and when we were kids we fought like any other brother and sister. I was such a mama's boy, a goody-two-shoes, and my sister was just so not. Also, my sister got busted every time she ate a grape in the supermarket. I, on the other hand, got away with murder because I saw my sister getting caught right and left, and I learned from her mistakes.

Dee Dee was a cheerleader and a track star in high school and a member of the dance squad in college—an amazing overall athlete. Everything comes so naturally to her. One good thing about having a sister is that I've always been comfortable around girls. She was the coolest chick in high school, so I was cool by extension. She always had a gang of cheerleaders over at the house, and I hit on them all, even though I was only in eighth grade. I'm sure they weren't thrilled to get a come-on from a middle-schooler, but as a result I've never been intimidated by beautiful women.

Later, when I started dating, I had the advantage over my buddies because women weren't this big mystery to me. I knew a little about what made them tick—like, a girl wants you to listen to her without interrupting when she's telling a story. She wants you to ask her questions about her life and not just brag about yourself. And when she's venting to you out of frustration, she doesn't want you to automatically try to fix whatever bad situation she's talking about.

But I guess all this insight at an early age didn't guarantee success—after all, it didn't help me open up in my marriage. I understood women slightly better than some, I suppose, but that didn't mean I knew what to do with that knowledge.

I had been confiding in Dee Dee all along about my marital problems, and she always had been a willing and able sounding board. But this time, I needed something different from her. When I told Dee Dee that Jennifer and I were splitting up, she started to say, "You know, I always thought the problem with the two of you was—" but I cut her off. I told her that this was nothing she or anyone could fix and that I just needed her to listen to me. And she really heard me, because she quickly shifted gears. She listened as I vented, she told me how much she loved me, and she promised that both she and J.D. would be there for me. It was great—exactly all that I needed to hear. That's just like people, though—if you're honest about your feelings, and if they're worth their salt, they will generally respond in kind. And Dee Dee and J.D. are two of the saltiest of the earth. If I ever doubted them—which I didn't—I had no doubts now.

But before I could get on with the nightmare that Valentine's Day would be, I needed to make another call—to my parents. I had told them in December—on Christmas Eve, in fact—that Jennifer and I were having some very serious problems. So I knew this wouldn't come completely out of the blue. But now I had to tell them that there was actually going to be a divorce and that it was going to be final very soon. This call was much harder to make than the one to Dee Dee.

"Hey, stranger," my dad said. He sounded concerned almost immediately.

"Would you get Mom?" I asked. "And then put me on speaker-phone so I can talk to you both at the same time."

"What is it? Is somebody sick?" my mom said, her voice getting louder as she came toward the phone.

"I haven't been doing too well," I told them. My voice wavered, and I took a deep breath. I didn't want to start crying and cause them any more worry than I had to.

Mom was alarmed. "What's happened? Is it Jennifer? Is she okay?"

I had to struggle to say it—to make the statement I thought I would never have to. "Jennifer and I are getting a divorce."

Saying the words filled me with an enormous sadness, but also with another emotion that I can't quite describe—it was some-thing like relief. As I've said before, naming something makes it real. Telling my parents about the breakup made me completely realize for the first time that Jennifer and I were no longer to-gether and most likely never would be again. It was yet another tiny step in my process of moving on.

I had expected my parents to react with shock and tears, but they didn't seem completely surprised by the news. They sud-denly started talking over each other:

"We'll be over as soon as we can."

"We'll do anything at all that you need—you know that."

"We could pick you up and bring you back here. You can spend the night. We'll figure this out."

Filled with gratitude and love for them, I wept silently on the other end of the phone. After a moment, they realized I hadn't responded to any of their offers.

"Honey, are you okay?" my mom asked.

"Tell us what we can do for you," my dad said.

I told them how much they meant to me and said I was sorry I had shut them out of my life in recent days. "What I really need right now is some time alone while I figure things out," I told them. "I have to muscle through this by myself."

I could tell they were anxious and uncertain, but they didn't push me. They didn't offer me all kinds of advice or try to get me to talk it out. And they respected my need to be alone. My parents were usually so opinionated about everything, so I really appreciated that they were able to be the silent, sympathetic presence I needed.

"You know where to find us," my dad said. "If you need anything at all, don't hesitate to call."

Before hanging up, my mom said something I really needed to hear at that moment: "Bobby, we have such faith in you."

■

THE NEXT WEEK, I found myself right back on the couch with a bento box of sushi and salad, with the television tuned to ABC. I couldn't understand why I was drawn back to *The Bachelor*. Perhaps I had had so much drama in my own life, it was a refreshing change to finally witness someone else's. It was pure escapism at a time when I needed to escape the most.

APRIL

I had a hunch that the young woman named Amanda was clearly a favorite with Alex. She was busty, and she dressed to show off her cleavage—she was actually quite voluptuous. Whether or not she'd end up being the one he gave the last rose to, he was definitely interested. But then I noticed that when he talked about her, he always talked about how great her body was and how she knew how to use it. I thought, *If Alex is judging these women only on looks, he isn't going to end up making the right choice.* That realization surprised me—after all, I'd always gone after gorgeous women, too.

The next morning as I rolled into work, the conversation again centered on *The Bachelor.* Someone mentioned that they thought Alex was being misleading at times—telling a girl he wanted to keep seeing her, but then not giving her a rose in the end. I felt he got away with it because after the rose ceremonies, the girls left the mansion and he didn't have to deal with the repercussions. That wasn't true for me and any of the women I'd ever dated. Midwestern women can be tough. If I led a woman on and then rejected her, I would wake up to find a horse's head in my bed.

■

NOW HERE WE WERE, in the middle of April, and Dee Dee called one day and said, "Let's grab a drink. We won't say a word about Jennifer unless you want to. We'll just be drinking buddies for the night. J.D. can babysit."

We agreed to meet at a martini bar that used to be our favorite watering hole, although I hadn't been there in ages.

When I saw my sister waiting for me at the bar, I felt like crying—I couldn't help it. The revelations I had made to her and my par-

ents had wiped me out emotionally and left me without the strength
to keep it together.

She led me to a back table and ordered us vodka martinis with
blue cheese–stuffed olives—two for each of us. After my first
drink, I was able to speak. We talked about what was going on in
her life, and about how her son was enjoying preschool. Then we
talked about the cottage that my parents owned on a lake in Northeast Michigan.

"Hey, let's make plans to spend a lot of weekends up there this
summer," she said excitedly. "We can have tons of parties." Then
she opened her mouth to say something else, but closed it again. I
knew what she was going to say. I loved the cottage but hadn't
been up there as much over the past few years, because of all the
demands. Now I could spend as much time there as I wanted.

I didn't say anything, so she continued. "We could bring a ton of
people and have barbecues. And we could get some good poker
games going. C'mon. Wouldn't some fierce competition and gambling be just the kind of excitement you could use right now?"

"Yeah," I admitted.

"Hey, do you remember how you and Mom and Grandma used
to go gambling at the casino?" Dee Dee asked.

"Sure." When I was still in the band, I also worked part-time in
advertising, and I had to commute between East Lansing and
Toledo, which is about four hours away. To cut down on some of
the driving, I'd stay at my parents' house every Tuesday night.
Mom and I would take Grandma gambling at a casino in Windsor,
Canada. I'd play roulette or blackjack. Grandma and Mom would
play the quarter slots.

APRIL

"It was pretty funny," I said. "Our own Tuesday-Night Gambling Club." I shook my head and laughed. It was good to have that happy memory of Grandma just then, when I was feeling so low.

Dee Dee and I were silent for a moment. I looked around the bar. In the corner a pianist was on his bench, playing bad tunes. The drink servers wore bow ties and paisley vests, and the man at the table next to ours lit a cigar and took several puffs.

"Jennifer would hate this place," I said, and I started to laugh.

Dee Dee put her hand over mine. She leaned in and said kindly, "Well, then it's good that it's just you and me."

■

MAYBE IT'S NOT so surprising that after I had reconnected with my family, I began to miss Jennifer's family, whom I loved and respected. Her dad was a man who came from very humble beginnings and never lost sight of who he was or where he had come from. He thought a lot about what he said before he said it. Her mother was beautiful and a little shy but gracious—with a great sense of humor. Her sister is as gorgeous as Jennifer, and fierce as a lioness when it comes to her family. Her husband was like a brother to me. I will always have the utmost respect for them, and I loved being part of their family.

I was present when Jennifer's niece and nephew were born, and I'd never missed a birthday or holiday with them until the time Jennifer and I split. The kids were very important to me and I realized, with appropriate chiding from Jennifer, that my sending gifts for birthdays, Easter, and what have you was only confusing the situation, not helping. But I fought it for some time.

I suppose I understand why Jennifer was so adamant. A clean

break would cause the kids less pain later. They needed to realize that Uncle Bob would no longer be around. *I* needed to understand that Uncle Bob would no longer be around. All throughout that month, Dee Dee's son Jack kept asking, "Where is Aunt Jennifer?" It broke my heart. I simply had to be honest and explain that she wasn't going to be around anymore. I imagine Jennifer must have had it worse with her sister's children, because I had been a big part of their lives. They were several years older, too, so I'm sure they had many more questions.

Also, what I didn't know at the time was that Jennifer was already seeing someone new. I guess having birthday cards arrive from the ex made the family too confused and uncomfortable, considering the new situation.

I still have a picture of Jennifer's niece and nephew up in my office, and I still have one up at home. I can't believe how much losing contact with those kids hurt me—and continues to.

■

I TOOK COMFORT wherever I could. And one comfort was my new routine of Japanese takeout and a dose of reality TV. On the day of the next episode of *The Bachelor,* I finished up work in order to get home in time for it. As I was putting on my coat at the end of the day, Greg popped his head into my office.

"Hey bud, want to grab dinner?"

"No thanks." I quickly groped for a lie. "I have to get home to meet the plumber." I cringed inwardly. What plumber comes by at seven at night? An awfully expensive one, I'll tell you that! Greg simply nodded and left. I had to face the fact that I was truly hooked.

On the final dates, I was drawn to the petite blonde woman

named Trista. I admired her sense of dignity as she shared a house with other young women who were dating the same guy she was—a situation that was so inherently undignified. I thought the way she kept saying that Alex had to listen to his heart was very wise. It got me thinking about how much I'd stopped listening to my heart in my relationship with Jennifer.

To be frank, watching the show made me realize that I was ready to share some of my affection with someone. There Alex was, in an elegant restaurant or in a hot tub, smooching a gorgeous woman, and here I was, alone in my living room, feeling out of shape, with my empty Japanese take-out box on the table.

I started thinking about Jennifer and wondering why we had lost our sense of intimacy with each other. It made me begin to think there was something wrong with me. I'm a healthy young guy. I love a roll in the hay as much as anybody. I mean, I was with this gorgeous woman, and it got to the point where we barely talked or even touched each other. I had to face the fact that although I found her beautiful, we didn't have that chemistry anymore—that indescribable "something." Greg and his wife sure have it. His wife says all the time, "He's such a hottie!" She actually has a T-shirt that says "Greg Clausen is a hottie," and she wears it with pride!

That's the goods—if you have that, you've got everything. Granted, they've only been married two years, but that's more spark than I had had in so many different ways.

At about this time—what should have been the worst time of my life—several of my best friends called to ask me what I was doing on an upcoming Friday. I told them that my only plan was a divorce. After the laughter and the tears subsided, they informed me that they were having a dinner party, and they were insistent that I come.

"I'm honestly not going to be up for it, guys," I told Melanie (Gregg's wife), Katie (Greg's wife), and Lynda (Kipp's wife), who were all on the line together. "I have no clue if I'm going to want to see anyone on that day."

"Are you crazy?" Katie fired back. "It's a divorce party! It's in your honor."

I couldn't believe it. It became apparent that the three of them had put together quite the gig for me to "celebrate" my newfound bachelorhood. And the gathering was no small affair. We went to a restaurant in Royal Oak called Andiamo and gathered at a table for more than twenty people. We shared happy memories, laughed hysterically, and talked about every possible topic, including . . . yes, *The Bachelor.*

In talking with everyone, I realized exactly how much I had missed out by not catching the first episodes of the show. I was surprised to learn from everyone how sexual Alex and Amanda had gotten on national television, but I had just as much fun talking about the shenanigans as everyone else did. Apparently, after their dinner date, they had taken over a hotel suite and ordered "Sex in the Sheets" from room service—ice cream, hot fudge, caramel, a Polaroid camera, and a plastic sheet. The last image everyone had seen was a Polaroid of Amanda, covered in chocolate syrup.

Katie said some things about the show that night that, strangely, I remember today. She remarked that a lot of the girls seemed like they were not there to make friends but just to win the guy. When I think about that, after my own experiences, I believe they were making a mistake. People who pass up a chance to make a friend—no matter the situation—always end up losing out. (Later, when I was on *The Bachelorette,* I and a lot of the other guys were there specifically to make friends and meet a great lady, and I believe that our camaraderie was a huge part of why the show was such a success—more appealing in a lot of ways, I think, than even that first series of *The Bachelor.*)

In the time following that wonderful evening, I made a point of catching the remaining episodes of the show. And I began to see that, although the program was meant to be entertainment, the people on the show were clearly experiencing very real feelings. At the end of one show I remember seeing clips of one of the women who didn't get a rose actually becoming so upset that she couldn't take a breath, and an ambulance had to be called.

Later, when I was on *The Bachelorette,* I would see firsthand how intense the feelings got—like the connection between Trista and Ryan. As it progressed, most of us didn't want to get in the way of it.

And I enjoyed watching Alex's date with Trista, which took place in Kona Village, Hawaii, when they took a helicopter ride and Alex ended up vomiting into an airsickness bag. Of course, seeing someone make a fool of himself on national television is always entertaining—that's half the reason we have reality shows in the first place. But, again, Trista's behavior was very classy. She took it in stride and didn't let it ruin their trip.

Still, despite all the barfing, Alex continued to come across like a slick guy, the country's most eligible bachelor—the complete opposite of me at the time, as I was feeling overweight and depressed, and was still harboring a tinge of pain and rejection. While the show was a diversion during a very difficult time, I didn't identify with it in any personal way. If you had tried to convince me during that bleak and lonely month of April that not only would I eventually recover from the devastation of my divorce, but that I would also one day be *The Bachelor,* selecting lovely ladies at rose ceremonies, I would have fallen out of my chair, laughing.

4.

◼

MAY

When everyone around you is saying bad things, sometimes
the strongest statement you can make is with silence.

IF APRIL WAS my month of family, May was my month of friends. My hand felt odd—too light without my wedding ring. And the house suddenly seemed very large and very empty. I suppose the finality of it all had set in, and, besides, I was coming up on what would've been my three-year anniversary. After a moment, I grabbed the phone off the wall and punched in my friend Kyle Steele's number.

"Hey, man," I said rather gloomily into the phone.

After hearing my voice, he asked, "Is everything okay?"

I simply said, "I don't think so."

Kyle lives about twenty-five minutes away from me, but he was at my house in about nine. I'm not kidding. He showed up looking a little windblown, with a bag of groceries—steaks, chicken breasts, chorizo, salads, you name it, and of course a bevy of video games, beverages (both alcoholic and non), and an attitude like he just pulled off something amazing.

"Fire up the grill," he said.

I smiled. "Thanks, man, but I'm not that hungry."

"So don't eat," he said. "Everybody else will."

"Everybody else?" I asked.

"Oh, I called a few people on my way over," he said as he went to put the groceries on the kitchen counter. "I said, 'Pass the word along—the party's at Guiney's. It's his anniversary.'"

Before I could protest, the doorbell rang. It was Greg and Katie, with a half gallon of vodka. Ten minutes later it rang again, and it was Dee Dee and J.D. Within a half hour, my backyard was filled with all my friends, eating steak and chicken off the barbecue and laughing and talking. My dear friend (and my band's bass player) Matt Jackson and one of our best boys Ozzy showed up with a guitar, and we sang some Journey tunes. Every single person found a chance at some point in the evening to come up to me and say quietly, in his or her own way, "I'm here for you." I had been so isolated, and then all of a sudden I felt this overwhelming rush of love being directed toward me.

While I was flipping chicken on the grill, my friend Kevin Donathan (whom I have known since we were in the first grade—he was my college roommate and the best man at my wedding) came over to talk to me, and we started joking and laughing. Dok is among the toughest people I know. Always has been. He is not the type of guy who sits around talking about puppies and rainbows. But as he walked over to me, he put his arm on my shoulder and suddenly burst into tears.

"What's wrong?" I asked him. "I'll be fine, bro." But he shook his head.

"They're tears of joy," he said, wiping at his face with his shirt-sleeve. "I've got my buddy back."

"What do you mean?" I asked. "I didn't go anywhere." But he said that I had. He said that I'd been so miserable, I'd become a shell of my real self. Now at least there was a chance for me to be happy again.

Unlike Kevin, I wasn't sure I believed that I actually would ever be that happy again. I was in the "love is for suckers" mind-set and planned to stay there for a while. But I couldn't help thinking that as long as I had these people with me along the way, my future couldn't be completely disastrous. I was having fun for the first time in months, but that's not what touched me most—what did was the confirmation that I had friends who would stick by me throughout those long stretches in life when there isn't any fun to be had.

The party was just what I needed. Unfortunately, shortly there-after the situation took a bad turn. When news got out about the divorce, people were shocked. As they approached Jennifer and me, we both felt pressured to explain what had happened. It was about this time that the rumor mill kicked in, and we began hear-ing strange things.

One night, three of my best friends and I went to a Pistons game. While there, we saw a young woman in the bleachers whom I'd dated while at the frat house in college, before meeting Jen-nifer. My buddy Kevin McCrone ("Weaz") mentioned laughingly to the other guys that he'd been in the bedroom next to mine and had to put a pillow over his head most nights, because of all the noise. And then he paused and added, "So, now that I think about it, it isn't true that Bob can't deliver."

I was shocked at what I was hearing. People were saying I couldn't perform in the sack? And once that one rumor was out in the open, they all started pouring out. The rumor mill had kicked out some doozies, and some of them directly conflicted with one another. My buddy Gregg Morrison ("Yam") mentioned that he had heard I was screwing around on my wife, among other things. To say the least, it was shocking! As much as it hurt to hear these things, my friends and I couldn't help but see the humor in it. We realized the contradictions.

I said, "So I can't deliver, and yet somehow managed to be unfaithful? How exactly does this happen?" Although we were able to joke about it after a long night of talking, it became apparent to me that the truth of a divorce is that hurtful things are often said, not necessarily by the key players, but by those who revel in others' business and misfortunes. My buddy Jeff Kipp said it best when he stated, "They attack you in ways you can't defend yourself. Regardless of what you say, you look too defensive." And he was exactly right.

I heard many terrible things about myself that night, and they were deeply hurtful and upsetting. The plus side was that once I knew which rumors were circulating about me, at least I had a chance to refute them. The challenge was finding ways to do so with my actions, without stooping to respond. Still, I couldn't believe that people would even say such things about another person, much less believe them.

The fact was that over the years my friends had become Jennifer's friends; they loved me, but they also loved her. Everyone got caught between two people who they both cared about, and they didn't know what to believe. Hearing friends talk about intensely private details of my life really hurt me to the core—and so much of the information was not true. I had no idea how things had gotten so wildly out of hand.

One day, a friend called me, so upset that I almost couldn't understand what she was saying. She had heard some of the rumors and was appalled. She wanted me to say bad things back about Jennifer, to even the playing field.

But I said I didn't want to. I felt that trashing Jennifer would invalidate what we had had together, which—at times—had been pretty remarkable. Granted, at other times it hadn't been so great. But I knew that refusing to take part in the mudslinging was the one thing that would allow me to maintain at least a small shred of dignity.

For the next few weeks, outrageous stories about me were passed around, snowballing as they traveled from person to person. Based on what they were saying, I was worse than the Unabomber. I was perverse and morally corrupt. I kept silent through it all. Refuting the allegations would have made me look defensive, and when you look defensive, you look guilty. When you respond to allegations, you validate them in a way. So in the end I just waited until it all blew over. One thing I did tell everyone was, "If you have something bad to say about Jennifer or about our marriage, don't say it in front of me."

I believed (and still do) that if you can't keep yourself from talking about the bad things your ex did, go see a counselor. But don't involve your friends and family. It's not fair to your ex or to anybody else.

MAY

■

JENNIFER AND I had been such a stable couple for so long (at least in everybody's eyes), and when a pillar of stability suddenly crumbles, the ground shifts under everybody's feet. As soon as they heard about our split, several other couples in our group started having problems, and some even said that our split had triggered the problems. It's the ripple effect.

After we broke up, my friends started coming to me for advice about *their* troubled relationships, but I wouldn't offer any—I would just hear them out in the same way I had just wanted to be heard. I had learned the importance of just letting someone talk.

One of the couples that split after we did was Kevin McCrone and his girlfriend. In fact, Kevin came to stay with me after the breakup. He didn't have anywhere to go, so he rented a room in my house. Kevin and his girlfriend had been together for two years, but their split was as difficult for him as Jennifer's and mine was for me.

"God, it's a killer, isn't it?" he asked me the evening he moved in. We were sitting on my back porch, drinking vodka tonics.

"What's that?"

"One day I'm waking up next to the woman I love, the next I'm here, having to look at your ugly mug."

I laughed. "Yeah. Who would have ever thought?"

We sat in silence for a moment.

"I guess I just never realized how unhappy Jennifer was," I said. "She says it should have been obvious, but I guess I didn't want to see it. Because if I saw it, then I'd have to do something about it."

"Yeah, I understand that," Kevin admitted. "Maybe you hoped

that if you didn't talk about what was happening, it wouldn't really be happening."

It was hard to talk about our relationships at first—guys really would much rather talk about anything else. But the longer he lived with me, the more we got used to it, and our talks helped me process some of what had happened.

■

AND INSIGHT HAD come from another person as well—someone I hadn't yet met and didn't know I ever would. At the end of April, *The Bachelor* had drawn to a close. I was shocked when Alex picked Amanda over Trista, and so were a lot of people throughout the country.

I remembered that at the end of the episode, when Trista was in the limo, driving away from Alex and wiping her tears, she said, "I just have to trust that he was not the right one. I have to have faith that my prince is out there somewhere." While that May—only one month after the divorce—I was not mentally in a place where I had even begun to pick up the pieces or been able to apply any new philosophy to my romantic life, somehow that statement stuck in my mind.

Eventually that concept—that the moment you're rejected by someone is the very moment you have to have faith that he or she was wrong for you and that the right person *is* out there—would become a cornerstone of my beliefs. And of course in Trista's case it was completely true. Alex was not the right man for her, and her Prince Charming *was* out there, waiting to meet her—along with twenty-four other guys, myself happy to be among them.

5.

◼

JUNE

Scars are what make us human.

SHAYRIKO

B Y THE TIME summer rolled around, I was still pretty much stuck. Time had passed, but I didn't really feel like myself yet. I was still doing physical rehab on my knee—in fact, I was doing a little too much.

"Careful," said a physical trainer, when he saw how hard I was tackling the exercise bike. "You don't want to overdo it."

But I had the crazy idea that my old life was just around the corner, and I could get back to it if I only pedaled hard enough. And I was throwing myself back into sports, too, with a vengeance. I jumped back into a basketball league and joined a softball team with some friends, as well as trying to work out as much as possible with my buddy Kipp at the Lifetime Fitness near his home in the mornings. But then one day, as I was playing softball, I was running around first base when I felt something pop, and I went down. There was a ripping sensation in the back of my leg, and a searing, burning pain. It turned out I had ruptured my Achilles tendon. After that I was right where I didn't want to be—back on crutches and extremely pissed off. It was incredibly frustrating.

The sad part was that I was back in the world again, yet I was still lonely. I think I really craved intimacy with someone. Not just a physical relationship, but some true intimacy. Part of getting your self-esteem back is proving to yourself that you're still attractive enough to the opposite sex. Flirting and sparking with someone is a great way to feel good about yourself, and also to let someone else feel good about herself with you. But I also think it's important to be able to feel a definite connection with someone, when everything doesn't have to be spelled out constantly. Where the unspoken works as well as the spoken. And that's what I was truly craving.

A woman named Shayriko who shared our office space was always trying to set me up with her friends. "C'mon," she said. "I know lots of nice girls who don't want anything serious. You could just have some fun."

"No blind dates. I can hardly face my friends—how could I face a stranger?"

We were sharing a roast beef sandwich in my office one day in May. She leaned back in her chair and crossed her right ankle over her left knee. She was a financial-planning analyst. She wore red lipstick that stood out against her pale skin, and her shiny black hair was always drawn back into a neat French twist, but she wasn't a priss—she was one of the guys, a member of the office baseball team, a beer drinker, a Pistons fan, and she had the loudest, most explosive laugh I've ever heard.

"Well, then I guess you'll just have to date me," she said. I choked, and she laughed.

So we started hanging out together outside the office. We'd go to midnight gigs at the Magic Bag in the middle of the week, party in the front row, and listen to bands we'd never heard of before. Or we'd pick up burgers and fries and make a picnic of it in Kennebec Park. Then we'd go back to my house and sit under a blanket in front of the unlit fireplace and talk about past relationships or watch some pay-per-view movies. It was plain old fun. She had no problem if I wanted to talk about Jennifer, or my marriage, or how I still couldn't make sense of what had gone wrong. Sometimes she stayed the night, and it was so comforting to have a warm body cuddled up beside me instead of being alone in my big bed.

"Sometimes I feel like I've been scarred for life," I said to her once. "I'm damaged goods."

"Did you know that the average American has three dozen scars on his body by the time he's seventy-five years old?" she asked. "Scars are what make us human."

She gave me something I hadn't had in years—complete acceptance. Our relationship was funky and fun, and she took it for what it was—just a chance for two people to enjoy each other. She was really instrumental in helping me regain my confidence. It was like, all of a sudden, boom! *I'm back! God, what a relief.*

In early June, after we'd gone out for a few weeks, she asked me to meet her after work for margaritas at a bar not too far from my house.

"Listen," she said, dabbing at the salt on the rim of her glass with the tip of her slender finger. She couldn't meet my eyes. "I think we need to talk."

I had to force myself not to clutch at my chest and fall off the barstool. Ladies, if you want to give a man a coronary, just say the words "We need to talk."

"I have been having a lot of fun with you, but I'm beginning to feel that I need more, emotionally, than what I've gotten out of our relationship," she continued, still not looking at me. "I think I need more of a commitment."

I took her hand. "You know where my life is right now. I've been honest from the start."

Then she did turn to look at me, and I saw that her dark eyes were full of compassion, and maybe even a little humor.

"I know, Bob. I actually mean . . . I'm seeing someone else."

"Oh." I was momentarily speechless. Then we both burst out laughing.

"I think I'm falling in love with my yoga instructor," she continued after our fit had subsided. "Last night we went on a date, and it seems like we could be a really good match. I'd like to give it a chance to work out." She squeezed my hand. "You don't mind, do you? I didn't want to hurt you after all you've been through."

Oddly, I did feel a tiny pang of loss, but it was quickly replaced by pleasure at the possibility of a good friend finding true love. At a time of so many endings, I was cheered to hear of a new beginning.

"I couldn't be happier for you." I leaned forward and kissed her cheek. "Can he put his ankles behind his ears?" I added, and she laughed so loudly that other guests of the bar turned their heads and stared. We laughed the rest of the night. The two of us had a real connection, real intimacy, and we would remain good friends.

■

So SHAYRIKO and I stopped seeing each other, and I started dating quite a bit in June. I went a little nuts. I was doing everything to excess—even my work. I would go into the office and stay for fifteen hours a day and then go out partying. It was really insane, but I couldn't get myself to slow down. In fact, I started making opportunities for myself to do things that I had never experienced before. On one weekend, J.D., my cousin Andy, a buddy named Billy C., and I loaded up the boat and took a leisurely ride down to Put-in-Bay in Ohio. I have to say that Put-in-Bay is a haven. A true spring break for grown-ups. And we had a blast! As luck would have it, I was still sporting my cast—which would remain a staple for the summer—and it was hilarious how it helped us get the best parking spots for our golf cart (cars aren't allowed on the island) and how outfitting the cast with a life vest of its own became comic relief for all of us. It was also a lovely conversation starter when meeting women. I began having a much better time adjusting to being a single man again. It wasn't an easy transition at first, but it was certainly becoming easier—and a lot more fun.

I happened to have a couple of buddies who had also recently gone through breakups, so they were in the same place that I was—trying to move on. We would all go out to the bars and make new friends and chat with the ladies. It was a momentary break from having to think about all the depressing stuff we'd been dealing with over the course of the last several months.

■

IT'S FUNNY to me when people attack *The Bachelor* or *The Bachelorette,* because they really show exactly the same things that take place in the real world every day: going to a bar or restaurant, meeting a bunch of strangers, and choosing the one you want to spend more time with. It's a complete mirror of what takes place on reality TV—it just isn't broadcast into everyone's homes across the nation, and you don't hand out roses.

Of course, one crucial difference is that the people on the TV shows have been prescreened. They've been tested for STDs, had background checks, and they have been analyzed for mental health issues. That isn't the case when you meet a new person in real life. So I guess in some ways reality shows are a damn fine way to meet someone.

Being out in the world was so refreshing after months of sitting alone in front of the television. I met a lot of women during this period. And I saw something beautiful in each of them—whether they were fitness trainers, college coeds, high-powered attorneys, or typists. I met women of all shapes, sizes, and ethnicities; I met women with colored contact lenses and women who wore thick glasses, women with perfect skin, and women whose faces showed the wear and tear of hard times—they were all beautiful.

Perhaps it was because I myself was now forty pounds heavier and eight years older than I had been the last time I was single. I couldn't help but see myself through their eyes—I was no longer the hot young singer in the band, fresh out of college. I had some mileage and, at the time, the spare tire to go with it. In fact, my buddy Dok would always laugh, asking if we were getting ready to go swimming. "Why?" I'd ask. "Because it looks like you've already got your inner tube on." Guys will joke with one another that way. And it made me laugh.

Maybe that's what gave me a sense that these women and I shared a common humanity. So many people had been wounded by life, whether or not I could see it on their faces. I wanted to know their stories. "What are you looking for in your life?" I'd ask them after we'd had a couple cocktails. Who was the love of your life? Do you still love him? Would you take him back? Honestly not a pickup line, just talking to them about everyone's favorite subject—themselves.

I would tell them my story, too. I made sure they knew so they wouldn't think I was leading them on. "Here is what has happened in my life and where I'm coming from. I'm not looking for anything serious. Most likely, I'm not looking for anything beyond this drink." I realize how funny I must have sounded to some of them—who did I think I was to presume that they wanted anything more from me?

If we seemed to have a real connection, sometimes I'd invite everyone back to my house with me for an after-party. Even if we didn't, I usually had the party anyway.

Sometimes the woman I was with would be a little hurt that I wasn't looking to get into a serious relationship with her. But a lot of times the woman found my situation refreshing and honest— which was probably worse. She wanted to take care of me, to get me through the ordeal—she wanted to keep seeing me, thinking she could change me.

What a lot of women don't realize is that where a guy is in his life has a lot to do with whether or not he wants to get into a relationship. If at that moment he is not looking for something serious, she could be the most fabulous thing in the world, but he's still not going to get involved. But it's the guy's responsibility to be clear. And I did my best to be.

Only once that I can recall did things get a little scary. I met this woman on a plane—a lingerie model from New York named Shelly. We had a drink together on her layover in the Detroit airport. Suddenly, she just leaned over and kissed me. We had been talking for fifteen minutes! The kiss kind of threw me, but I tried to play it cool and not show my feelings.

Shelly had an international background—she had been born in Dublin and worked for several years in Zurich. She had a master's in psychology from New York University, as well as the most gorgeous set of legs I've ever seen. We exchanged numbers, and I thought, *Hey, this could be fun.*

But after just a couple phone calls, I realized that something wasn't right. She started saying "I love you" and sending me poems. Then I got a call from her saying that she missed me and really needed me and wanted me to come to New York. At that point, I knew there was a problem. I mean, we'd had only a brief encounter, and she was talking like we were in a long-term relationship. Finally I had to leave her a long message that said, "I'm not feeling the same things for you that you are for me. I don't want to pursue this." I felt bad leaving the message, but I had to do it. Otherwise I thought I might end up with Glenn Close in my house, attacking me with a kitchen knife.

But to be honest, my biggest fear during this time was not a fear of a *Fatal Attraction*–type scenario. My fear was that I would meet "the one." It was just the wrong time in my life. I was scared of falling for someone, because I wasn't in a place where I could do anything about it. I used to say, "I hope I don't meet someone amazing." I was scared that, because of my emotional state, I would unwittingly pass over a woman that I was truly meant to be with.

■

GOING FROM BEING a faithful husband to being a single man back on the dating scene was an enormous adjustment. But once I got used to it, I realized that life can get better after a huge change. And that makes you less fearful of the next change that might come along.

This period proved something my family always said was true— you don't have to have all the answers before you start moving forward. You'll never know all the answers anyway. Fooling yourself into waiting until you do know them will keep you mired in a bad situation.

Now I love change. I welcome it into my life. I love shaking things up, rocking the boat, throwing a wrench in the works. It's good for you, and it opens your life to more possibilities, new chances, and new opportunities.

6.

◼

JULY

*You have nothing truly meaningful to offer anyone else
until you've learned how to give to yourself.*

O NE HOT AFTERNOON in July, I was sitting in John's office
without a whole lot to say. He sat across from me with a
mild look on his face. His peach-colored office with the soft couch,
coffee table, and pale watercolor paintings had become so familiar.
The odd thing was that even after all these months of coming to
see him, I couldn't tell if I was getting any better.

"I'm making progress, right?" I asked him.

"Well, what do you think?" he asked.

I sighed. "I don't know. Some days I'm sure I am. Other days, I
still feel as bad as I did the day Jennifer walked out the door."

He leaned back in his chair and smiled.

"That's perfectly normal," he said. "We live in a fast-track culture where everything is so linear, like a rise up the corporate lad-

der. But getting through a grieving process is more like climbing a steep sand dune—it's two steps forward, one step back."

We sat in silence for a moment.

"What do you want for yourself?" he asked.

My response was immediate. "I want my life back before everything got so screwed up. I was so happy the way things were. I want to get there again."

He looked at me with an amused glint in his eye.

"What if you had the choice between that life and a totally different one?"

I was caught a little off guard by the question.

"Your life doesn't have to be the same," John explained. "Think of your life as a house and the divorce as an earthquake. Now your house is in rubble. You need to rebuild the house, but you don't have to redo it just the way it was. You might choose to rebuild it differently."

It was a daunting idea, but also exciting. Clearly, since my life had gone so terribly wrong, there must have been things that needed fixing. I felt like I had dug enough of the rubble away that I could finally start thinking about what to do next—I could build a new, better, stronger house. I forced myself to face some hard truths about my old life. It was difficult, but I knew I had to do it, if only to learn from the pain so that I'd never have to go through it again.

My first decision was to stop trying to please everyone.

Jennifer had once said to me, "In business, you're aggressive. You can make good decisions, and you don't let what people think or feel overshadow what you know to be the best choice. But in your personal life, you don't do that." I knew now that it was true. I needed to start applying some of my business attitude to the rest of my life. I began by thinking about my relationship with my parents. Without a doubt, they are great parents. They always put their children first. They never punished us if we behaved badly—they just expressed their disappointment. But that can be worse sometimes. I realized that I would do anything to avoid disappointing them. As a result, I let that dictate some of my actions instead of trying something else instead. It wasn't their fault—it was mine.

The whole "winners never quit, and quitters never win" mentality was big to me when I was growing up. While this sounds like a good way of thinking, in reality, it can backfire. It can force you to stay on a sinking ship when all your instincts are telling you to jump overboard.

When I was a kid, I was on track to be the youngest Eagle Scout in the state of Michigan. But the truth was that I didn't particularly want to be the youngest Eagle Scout in Michigan. My parents never pressured me, they only encouraged me, but I knew their expectations, so I put pressure on myself. As a result I ended up spending years of my time on something I didn't really want to do, when I could have been doing something that I actually did.

I did the same thing all over again in college, when I stayed on the football team much longer than I should have. The summer after my freshman year, I got a job at the steel mill, making camshafts and other motor parts. I was carrying a railroad tie on my back across the yard (which was a really stupid move), and I hurt my back really badly. For a long time, I couldn't even bend over and touch my toes. It screwed me up for the next football season and I think led to some of my subsequent knee injuries. By my junior year, I really didn't want to go out on the field anymore, but of course I had the whole "never quit" adage in my head, so out I went. Finally, after one more wasted season, I had the wisdom to call it quits. It just wasn't worth all the pain and exhaustion so I could say I was on the team.

Now, in the aftermath of the divorce, I was still trying to please everyone at the expense of my own needs. The same kid who couldn't leave the Boy Scouts became the man who couldn't allow his marriage to end. Luckily, my ex-wife believed differently. She was from the "if it sucks, get out" school.

When my family wanted something, and Jennifer wanted something, and her family wanted something, I didn't even consider what I wanted—in truth, I didn't have a clue as to what would please me. I would just take what everyone wanted and split it three ways. And, to be totally honest, I would put Jennifer's split third. I would think, *Well, I'm just going to try to make our parents happy, and Jennifer will understand.* And that must have made life hell for her. I always figured that she and I would have the rest of our lives to do everything we wanted, so what we wanted could wait.

Holidays were definitely the worst. I mean, what do you do when two different families want you to be with them on Christmas morning? In the end, every Christmas would be a real mess. I would kill myself, traveling breakneck speed all over the state, trying to get from one house to another. It was no one's fault but my own.

I needed to set some boundaries, but I didn't start doing that until after my divorce. I knew I should start with my family, since I was closest to them.

First, I decided that I couldn't announce to anyone that I was changing my behavior—I didn't feel the need to explain myself. Next, I decided not to make myself so available all the time. Usually,

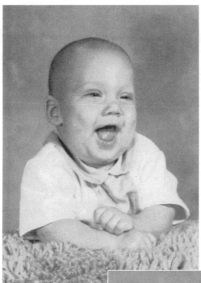

Obviously, I was a happy child.

Ah! Sears Portrait Studio. This shows my patriotism, even at a young age. USA! USA!

As evidenced here, some things never change. I'm still in desperate need of a haircut at all times!

As you can see, there's a vacuum in the lower right-hand corner of this shot. I was big into cleaning even then. I'm really bad about that—I'm the guy who starts cleaning up before the party is even over. I'm extremely meticulous . . . some say anal.

Hanging out on the sofa with my dad. Thankfully, my parents have gotten new furniture.

This is my favorite picture—it's my dad with my sister and me. He still looks the same now, more than twenty-five years later.

*Evidence that I hated to
mow the lawn even
then . . .*

. . . but I am into landscaping.

My parents planted a tree in our front yard when my sister was born, and one when I was born. My sister's tree grew to be huge—it's like the Christmas tree at Rockefeller Center. I'm shown here next to my tree. It's the same size today! I think I got ripped off, as mine is more like Charlie Brown's Christmas tree.

My first aqua jumpsuit. The first of many. However, please note the prowess on the catwalk, even then.

I still remember how uncomfortable this shirt was. I hated it. The trees in the background are actually on one of those screens they pull down behind you at the studio.

This is what happens when I try to dress myself. My mother dressed me the rest of the way through grade school. Sadly, that is not a joke. This was 1977. I think I wore a jacket just like that on Good Morning America *recently.*

The "double exposure" photo. We all have one! The main shot is that of a smiling, happy youngster. The second is far more contemplative and brooding.

The first year I played football, 1980. It was Freshman Little League football and we were the Peanut Bowl Champs. My business partner, Greg, actually QB'd us to victory that year!

I'm in fifth grade. That necklace I'm wearing is my father's "medic alert" chain for high blood pressure, which I'd found in a kitchen drawer. I thought it was the coolest thing. I wore it all the time.

Senior year in high school. My grandmother called this "the poodle 'do." I wore it tight on the sides, short in the back . . . and "poodley" on top! Some other guys had mullets. It was the eighties, so this really isn't that bad.

*This is my freshman year
in college, 1989. My Uncle
Big Red played football at
Michigan State, and I'd
always wanted to follow
in his footsteps.*

*This is a photo of me and my mom at the
Tigers game this year. This was the night
before my Mom's birthday, so I had them
put her name up on the Jumbotron. I love
Detroit sports!*

if there was a family get-together or a gathering of friends, it was assumed that everybody would be there, prior engagements or not. But now if I had made another plan, I would stick to it, even if that plan was to stay home alone and rent a movie.

It felt weird the first few times I actually put my plan into motion, partly because it made me realize how much I hadn't been firm with them in the past. This threw me so much that I actually overcompensated and was firmer than I'd planned to be.

Naturally, I worried about hurting my family's feelings and damaging our relationship, but what was remarkable—and John predicted that it would happen—was that the distance made my relationship with them stronger. We all began to respect one another's time and one another's lives, and when we all did get together, we cherished the event all the more—we were there because we truly wanted to be with one another and not just because it was expected.

Anyway, I'm more independent now. Recently, Dee Dee said to me, "This isn't fair. We've switched places, and I don't like it." I laughed, but it was true. I had been the mama's boy and she the wild child. And now I had made a change in my life and was starting to do all the things that I wanted to do, for me! She now had a baby and was living near and working with my mom and dad. She spent a lot more time with our family, and her own, while I was out and about. She had become the one hearing about me being such a rebel all the time.

"I want to be the rebel again!" she said. "What the hell happened?"

What happened was that, for the first time in my life, I was taking a stand. I realized that at times it's okay to be a bit selfish—as long as it is not at the expense of others and it works for your own betterment.

■

I ALSO REALIZED that I hadn't really grieved for my loved ones who had died. I wouldn't talk about my sadness, so I couldn't really get through it properly, and that added to my emotional distance. That's why the divorce hit me so hard—it was like I was grieving for several different things and people at once.

Another decision I made at that time was to curb my contact with Jennifer. We had been together for eight years—I just couldn't fathom how you could go from speaking to somebody every day for eight years to suddenly not speaking to them at all. I had this desire to keep everything friendly. But the more I looked back on it, the more I realized I wasn't protecting myself. I was putting myself in a position to get hurt, and then I did get hurt.

We would meet for coffee at Starbucks, and I'd tell her how I'd seen her modeling in a magazine or local newspaper, or how I'd heard about one of her business ventures. It was difficult because I would realize with sadness that I was not a part of her life. She would talk about a movie she had seen or a jazz club she had been to, and it was clear that she had done these things with someone she was involved with romantically.

If you've really loved someone, maybe you just can't be best friends afterward. Friends, but not best friends. And even being a friend may take some time. It can't be immediate. At least it couldn't be with me. People need distance—or at least I did.

JULY

■

I DON'T KNOW what I would have done without my shrink. His help at the time was instrumental to my recovery. When I wanted to take the blame for my failed marriage and the issues I had with family and friends, he said, "It's not about blame; it's about taking responsibility."

He allowed me to take responsibility whenever it was legitimate, and then steered me clear when I was trying to take responsibility for things that were out of my control.

I wish all counselors were as good as mine. In my opinion, some counselors seem to encourage their clients not to take responsibility for anything and instead cast the blame onto other people. But I don't think that helps a person. It might feel better in the moment, but if you don't acknowledge the part you played in something, you can never admit your mistake, forgive yourself, and move on.

I think it's kind of like that with the death of a loved one—if you don't grieve the death fully at the time and face the horror of the moment, you can't get better and feel happiness later. If you try to make these things too easy on yourself in the moment, they'll come back to haunt you.

Divorce made me relearn what it meant to feel happiness. Now I know I need to make myself happy first before I can really make other people happy.

I knew I wasn't totally there yet in terms of being ready for the next person in my life, but I was getting there slowly—someday I'd be able to open my heart again.

■

THE FUNNY THING IS, even though I've learned to see beyond the "winners don't quit, and quitters don't win" philosophy, I still think there's a hell of a lot to be said for determination and a willingness to stick things out. What's different now is that I also see that there's something to be said for an ability to let go and move on.

Also, around that same time, I passed another important milestone. I told John that I thought I would try to wing it for a while and see if I could go it alone, without him holding my hand. In other words, I wasn't going to be coming to see him anymore. It was a hard statement to make—typically, I had the oddest fear that it would hurt his feelings. But he wasn't hurt at all. He actually told me that I was more than ready to be out there figuring things out for myself. He was proud to let me go.

Now I don't worry so much about pleasing other people. I understand that I have to do what's good for me, and if sometimes other people are disappointed, so be it. And that feels pretty damn good.

The truth is that a winner can quit—if something is really not right—and still be a winner. And in the end, I think that's the lesson my family had always wanted me to learn. It just took me a while to figure it out.

7.

◼

AUGUST

You can't play not to lose—you have to play to win.

IN AUGUST I packed everything up and left for my family's cottage, which is out on a remote point in Northeast Michigan. Going there has always been a very grounding experience for me. With all the upheavals that life inevitably sends, it's been wonderful to have something so constant in my life.

It is particularly special because it reminds me of my Grandma and Grandpa Guiney, to whom I was always extremely close. When my sister and I were kids they would take us to the cottage for weeks on end. We'd sing by the campfire and take long walks in the woods. My grandfather, who is now gone, loved to take me fishing. When I am there, I often sense that he is there with me in spirit.

I call it a cottage, but it has seven bedrooms and three bathrooms. Still, it's very rustic. Not too far into the future I'd be spending six weeks with a bunch of other guys in a house that was just as big, except it had a pool, a hot tub, a game room, and two dining rooms—but the guys' house had nothing on the cottage, which is, I think, the most beautiful place on the planet.

The cottage had once been an old railroad station. When I was three, my parents bought it and my dad and grandpa rebuilt it by hand. A few years ago, we added a huge garage. My dad is a complete workaholic, and he refuses to let people help him because he can do a better job alone. On the garage, though, my buddy Matt and I were actually able to help my father build it, which was a hell of a lot of work. In fact, I did enough heavy labor during that summer to last a lifetime. Or at least that's my excuse now when I can't get there to help out as much.

The best memories of my childhood are from my time at the cottage. When I was five, I learned how to water-ski. I probably learned to fish even earlier. By the time I was nine, Dee Dee and I believed we had explored every inch of the surrounding woods. Dee Dee was a real tomboy as a kid, and together we were a pair of little savages, always sunburned, our feet constantly dirty. We were each other's favorite playmates, and yet we fought like cats and dogs.

My dad piloted small planes, and when I was little he and I would fly in low, buzzing over the lake so that the family would know to come pick us up at the local airport. It was actually a grass landing strip called South Branch Airport. It was an old cow pasture that had been turned into a landing strip. But, as with everything, my dad would navigate perfectly, and whoever was waiting at the house would come and pick us up.

That August, I spent a lot of time with my sister and J.D. on their boat as well—a beautiful powerboat with a cool aft cabin below deck. We took the boat out on the Great Lakes, which are so huge it's like being in the middle of the ocean—the shore is so far away, you can't even see it. Summertime in Michigan is amazing because of all the lakes, both inland and the Great Lakes. It's largely why I love the state so much.

Every weekend I would pick up friends in my Yukon and drive them up to the cabin—in fact, the only reason I bought such a large vehicle is that it could seat so many people.

Just as we'd done as teenagers and then as college students, J.D., Dee Dee, and I threw "cottage parties"—twenty or thirty people at the house, tents on the beach, a total blowout. We grilled steaks and ribs and corn. I am not a big fisherman myself, but a lot of my friends are, and they love the lake because the fishing is so good. So there was usually some fresh catch—bass or walleye—to throw on the grill as well.

My friends would bring their friends, so I was meeting lots of new people, albeit in a slightly more relaxed atmosphere than the bars and nightclubs. A lot of the women were quite young—in their early to mid-twenties—and they still seemed to be in that phase of just wanting to have fun.

One weekend I hit it off with a cute girl named Marisa who was a senior at Michigan State and a friend of my buddy Kyle. She came to sit and watch as I played volleyball on the beach and then later came to chat when I was manning the grill, so I had the feeling that maybe she liked me. Later, as we sat around a fire on the sand and kicked back on blankets, Marisa talked to Dee Dee about her sorority at Michigan State. Then she asked Dee Dee what I'd been like when I was a student there.

AUGUST

"Backup quarterback on the football team," said Dee Dee, proudly. "Social director of his frat house. An awesome singer in a great band. Just an all-around great guy."

"Oh, please," I said with a laugh. My sister was being a bit kind in her descriptions.

"Sounds like a guy I knew," said a redhead on the other side of the fire, who I hadn't really met at that point. There was an edge to her voice. "Big man on campus. Out for number one."

I had the feeling that she'd had her heart broken by such a guy, so I took a swig of my drink and didn't take it personally. But Dee Dee, ever loyal, took the bait.

"That isn't what my brother's like at all," she protested. "He's always cared about other people, to a fault."

The redhead didn't say anything, but gazed out into the darkness toward the water. We all realized that she'd had a few too many Cuba libres, and, besides, the cottage is no place for that type of attitude. In any event, her not responding sent the message that maybe she wasn't convinced. Or anyway Dee Dee must have thought so, because she cleared her throat and then said, "Let me tell you all a story about what happened in high school between Bob and a girl named Debbie."

"Oh, Dee Dee, please don't tell this story," I said, but I knew that once she got started, there was no stopping her.

"There was a girl in our high school named Debbie who had problems with her legs," Dee Dee began. "One spring, both Bobby and Debbie were on the track team. I don't know why a girl with a disabled leg would want to be on the track team, but she did."

The fire crackled and popped, and J.D. began working on his

fireworks display. He rolled his eyes and smirked at me because we'd all heard this story a thousand times.

"Well, one day, there was a track meet, and Debbie was on the track," said Dee Dee. "Of course, she couldn't run very fast, and after everyone else had gone over the finish line, she was still out on the track, struggling.

"Well, members of the other team started heckling her and calling out mean things, and she started to cry. But still, she kept running as best she could. And then, all of a sudden, I looked down and there was Bobby, running right next to her on the inner track, trying to motivate her to keep going. And then, before I knew it, our entire track team was down on the track, running alongside her and calling out encouragement. And when she finally crossed the finish line, the people in the bleachers just went wild."

There was a pause, and we could hear the gentle waves breaking on the shore of the lake. Then J.D. lit the hem of Yam's shirt on fire accidentally, and he waved it wildly, trying to put out the flames. I leaned my head back and looked up at the stars, laughing.

"That's a great story," said Marisa. After a moment, she came over and sat next to me, and I asked if she'd like me to make her a drink. Later, we took a long walk along the edge of the lake and hung out and kissed on the deck of the boathouse down the street.

■

MEETING PEOPLE at the cottage helped me let down my guard a little. I ended up seeing some of the girls again, back in Detroit. Others I didn't. But what I realized during the month of August was that my heart was really starting to heal in the tiniest of increments. Not that I was ready to love again—not by a long shot. I still wasn't sure if I'd *ever* really love again. But I no longer felt that the overwhelming pain of my divorce completely defined who I was as a person.

One weekend, a friend brought a guest—a tall and stunning woman named Claudia who worked as a publishing attorney. She was intelligent and charismatic, and she seemed just so put together.

One afternoon, as everybody else was Jet Skiing or playing volleyball in the water, Claudia and I decided to take a boat out onto the water for a booze cruise. We found a quiet, secluded inlet, and then killed the motor. She opened the cooler, which she'd packed with supplies to make Long Island iced teas and vodka tonics.

"So, Bob, you seem like such a nice guy," she said after a moment, a little flirtatiously. "Why hasn't some girl snapped you up?"

"One did," I said between sips. "But then she dropped me."

Claudia looked up at me, startled.

"I'm divorced," I explained, trying not to make eye contact. Even after all this time had passed, I hated having to say that word—*divorced*. It was embarrassing, and I glanced over at Claudia to see her reaction. She was smiling sadly.

"So am I," she said. "Since a year ago." She took a sip of her Long Island iced tea.

"Really?" I was surprised—she looked like everything a man would want.

She nodded. "It was awful. Everybody thought we had the perfect marriage and these great careers. All my girlfriends would say to me, 'You don't know how lucky you are. Your life is perfect.' That made it so much worse when I had to tell them we were splitting up. It was mortifying to admit that the so-called 'perfect life' they admired so much was actually a disaster."

She paused. I offered her some pretzels out of the bag I was working on, but she shook her head. Then she asked, "How do *you* deal with the embarrassment of being divorced?"

"I have no idea," I told her. I shifted back in my seat and propped my legs up on the boat's rail. "I've only been in the mix of divorce for six months, and sometimes I think I'll never know the answer to that question. I've always hated to admit failure."

We sat for a moment in silence and enjoyed the gentle swaying of the boat. A seagull flew overhead, and I watched it circle and then started to laugh at a memory of my grandfather—who hated seagulls—calling one a "flying rat."

"Forgive me if this is too personal," I said, "but what went wrong with you and your ex?"

Claudia cleared her throat and then said quietly, "The worst thing that could have possibly happened."

I looked at her. "He was unfaithful?"

She shook her head. "He had been acting distant and distracted for quite a while. At first, of course I suspected he was having an affair. It's the first thing you think of. But it turned out that he wasn't—something else was going on." She paused, her face heavy with sadness. "One day, he came home and said to me, 'I'm sorry, Claudia. But I just don't love you anymore.'"

I sat back up. I was stunned. Jennifer and I had had our problems, but the love we felt for each other was never in question.

Up until that point, I had been feeling that my divorce was the worst tragedy that could have happened to me. Was it possible that it could have been even worse? As Claudia poured us more drinks,

I realized that it could have been—Claudia was proof of that. The person who meant the most to you in the world could just fall out of love with you.

Funny, pondering the worst-case scenario made me feel better about what actually did happen.

She paused and wiped her hands on a bar towel. "So, how about you? What went wrong?"

I shook myself out of my reverie and gave her question some thought. "I screwed up," I said finally. "I lost the best thing I ever had."

"What do you mean you 'screwed up'?"

I took a deep breath. It was so much harder to explain than her situation. "Well," I said finally, "my old football coach would have said I was playing not to lose."

She cocked her head. "I don't know anything about football. What does that mean?"

"Well, in football, or any sport for that matter, I've seen teams play not to lose all the time. Being complacent or settling for status quo. Then, all of a sudden, they're down a couple of points, there's no time left on the clock, and they're sunk." I paused. "Do you get it?"

She nodded.

"Being too conservative can definitely backfire," I continued. "And I was too conservative in my marriage. By just trying to keep things from falling apart, I was willing to settle for something that wasn't great for either of us."

Claudia was quiet, but she smiled in a way that let me know she might know what I was talking about. At that point she told me, "I've realized that I want to be someone's favorite thing to do. Someone's favorite everything in a relationship." It made perfect sense. We sat for a moment, feeling how the pleasant warmth of the afternoon sun was offset by the mild breeze on the lake. Then Claudia leaned over the edge of the boat and skimmed her fingers in the water.

"Wow," she said. "The lake is the perfect temperature. Mind if I take a dip?"

I laughed. "Not at all. In fact, I'll be right behind you."

She stripped down to a red one-piece swimsuit and then did a perfect jackknife off the boat's stern.

■

AFTER MY TALK with Claudia, I thought a lot about the idea of "playing not to lose." One thing that Jennifer taught me by insisting on the divorce is that people should pursue fulfillment. Every person deserves to have top priority in his or her spouse's life, and if you're willing to accept less than that, you just aren't living life in the way it's meant to be lived. At least that's what I want to have in a relationship. And that's what I need to give, in order to get it back in return.

Instead of both of us working to make the marriage better, we got caught in the rat race, and it's like Lily Tomlin said, "The problem with the rat race is that even if you win, you're still a rat."

I can't speak for Jennifer, but during my marriage, I had been stuck in a daily grind. Work, work, work. Make money, make money, make money. At the end of the day, I was so tired I couldn't do something fun with her, like go for a walk. I'd come home and put on my pajamas and watch TV. It sucked, not just for Jennifer, but for me, too. I would work out maybe once every two or three weeks, and that's just about how often Jennifer and I would make the time to be intimate with each other. Our bodies and our minds are inexorably tied together, and if you are not being physically and mentally intimate, your mental health is going to suffer.

I was stuck in the "play not to lose" mentality. But I've learned my lesson. I am never going to be in that situation again. You pay too high a price.

■

IN AUGUST, a very important thing happened—I finally got off my crutches. While my mended Achilles tendon was still very tender, and I couldn't yet participate in all the sports that I loved—basketball, waterskiing, and general goofing around—at least I could start to walk like a normal person again. What a relief. You really don't realize how much you take for granted the ability to do something simple like go up a set of stairs until you have it taken away from you.

So, by the end of that summer, in more ways than one, my steps were shaky, but I was proud to once again be moving forward all on my own.

8.

◼◻

SEPTEMBER

The worst plan acted on is better than the best plan never put into action.

GRANDPA GUINEY

I N THE MIDWEST, by the fall, there's a real tang in the air, and you definitely know that winter is on the way. There's a beauty in the seasons changing in Michigan that you have to see to believe. But this particular fall brought something else, too—an experience that was so off the wall and ridiculous that I'm still amazed that I even considered it. The experience was, of course, *The Bachelorette.* I was never sure what would come of it or even if it was a good idea, but I always remembered what Grandpa Guiney said—that doing anything at all is better than doing nothing. He was always willing to wing it, even if he wasn't sure what the outcome was going to be. So when this opportunity came along, I decided to do the same.

It wasn't the first time I had dumbed my way into something successful. Years back, when I was still part of Fat Amy, I had heard an ad for a music contest on the radio, and the winner would get to record a CD for free. I didn't think we had much of a chance because we would be going against bands way more seasoned than we were. We wrote original music, but we were mostly a cover band, and we'd been together for only a year. But I love going for the long shot, and I knew that we had nothing to lose.

I sent in a demo tape of our ten original songs, and, to our shock, we won. We got to compete in a contest in Grand Rapids, Michigan, and the prize was the chance to record a CD for free. This gave us a chance to be heard by people in the music industry. After releasing this CD, which I admit was not an amazing product, we became well known and began advancing in our ability to write songs and draw crowds. As a result, we ended up with an offer from MCA music publishing. It was a publishing deal, not a record deal, but it was a big deal to us.

After all that transpired from entering something on a whim, I realized that winging it can sometimes gain huge rewards. So that's why I decided to go on *The Bachelorette* when I was offered a spot on the show. The funny thing is, the whole idea wasn't even mine in the first place.

In September, Beeba and Janaya, two young women who worked in my office, approached me in the break room. We would always discuss the women I was dating, and Beeba and Janaya would give me their opinions on these ladies. Generally speaking, they thought they could do better for me.

"If we were to set you up on a date, would you go?" Beeba asked.

"Maybe," I said. By this time, I was more open to the idea of a blind date than I'd been when Shayriko had first suggested it.

Then Janaya said, "Remember Trista, from *The Bachelor?*"

"Of course," I said. "She was a doll."

I assumed that they were planning to set me up with a woman who looked like Trista, and I forgot about it. But unbeknownst to me, Beeba and Janaya went straight to *The Bachelorette* website and entered a long bio about me, including photos from my band's website.

When I got a call from ABC, I didn't take it seriously. Greg and I had a long history of faking each other out with prank telephone calls. I mean, let's face it—writing out a mortgage can be pretty boring, and it's natural to come up with distractions. Ours was making fun of each other—and sometimes playing pranks on each other. Once I called him and convinced him I was April, his "girl-friend" from ninth grade, whom he claims he never dated, calling to get rates for a mortgage! I actually had him thinking I was her. I'm not really good at doing impressions. But strangely, I've faked him out several different times.

So when I got a call from a woman saying that she was Lacey, a casting producer from ABC, I was like, "Yeah, right." I was sure it was Greg. I hadn't applied to be a cast member, so why would ABC be calling me? Here I was, still feeling overweight and just this side of miserable—and I'm getting a call from *The Bachelorette*? Like I'm an eligible bachelor? I didn't believe it for a minute.

Assuming it was a joke, I gave Lacey a really hard time. When she said, "Do you think you could send us a video of yourself?" I said, "No, I don't think that I could do that at all." She called me several times, and I was always a wiseass.

I didn't realize it was a bona fide phone call until Lacey asked if she could call me back, and I said, "Let me call you." She gave me her number, and when I called her back I realized she really was with *The Bachelorette*! I had been a jerk to her for three days, and she had no idea why. Later, I had a chance to explain, and we laughed about it. She said that oddly, my attitude interested her and had actually compelled her to keep calling me back.

In any event, they asked me to send a video, but I still wouldn't do it. I didn't want to be the fat guy getting out of the shower for the blooper reel, like, "Hey, Trista. How about a piece of this?" But they liked me and wanted to see me anyway. I felt like they were responding to my upbeat character, and that gave me a boost at a time when I really needed one.

They faxed me a seventy-page application form. It held up the fax machine for half an hour, and I kept having to put in more paper. It was overwhelming. But they wanted to know all about me, and that seemed reasonable. After all, it's in the network's best interest for there to be a match—everyone's hoping for a proposal at the end, so they really try to bring together people who would be compatible. I spent several hours filling out the form, answering questions such as whether I had ever had a restraining order against me (no) or whether I had ever been convicted of a crime (no) or whether I had ever been married (yes).

Flying to Southern California to meet the producers was a novel experience. The producers were really funny, and we laughed a lot together. I had the feeling that they liked me. Still, I didn't think they were going to take me. They could see that I wasn't the supermodel type.

So after the interview, I did what anybody would do—I put on my swimming trunks, shades, and flip-flops, and went down to the pool. I ordered up some drinks and struck up a conversation with some of the girls there. We ended up singing some old Journey tunes together at the top of our lungs and having a great old time being loud and crazy. Then we turned around and saw that some of the producers were watching us. They asked me to come back up and talk to them some more. So I did, still in my swim trunks and flip-flops.

When I got the call that I was one of twenty-five guys chosen to be on the show out of thousands of applicants, I was *really* flattered. I decided that whatever would happen, I would just have the best time that I could. At the same time, by Detroit standards, competing with twenty-four other guys for a pretty girl isn't a TV show, it's an ass-kicking. So getting the girl wasn't my only goal. I also wanted to have fun and do something new.

There was actually only a three-week period between when I got asked to be on the show and when I left for taping. Maybe I was a last-minute add—I don't know. Anyway, I didn't tell anybody that I was going to do the show—not my friends, not my family. For one thing, I had signed a confidentiality agreement, so I didn't know if I was even allowed to let anyone know.

■

LIKE ANY KID, I dreamed of being a star when I was growing up. The irony is that even though I once had dreams of stardom, my appearance on the show had nothing to do with any thoughts about a career in entertainment. After all, by that point I already had a well-established career. I wasn't looking to cast that aside to work in Hollywood. And I'm still not. But I simply needed something new in my life. I needed my epiphany, and here it was.

My mother always said, "The brightest star shines even brighter when it takes other stars along with it." That has always stayed with me. I took it to mean that a whole galaxy is so much brighter than a single star. So if you take people with you and help make others look better, you'll shine brighter as well. So before I left for filming, I decided to enter into this new experience with a real team-player mentality. I didn't want to make anyone look bad—instead, I thought we could all end up looking good. And in the end it paid off, because—with a few marked exceptions—most of us did.

9.

◼

OCTOBER

Don't judge your insides against other people's outsides.

FROM A YOUNG AGE, I learned to be comfortable in crowds. When I was growing up, my parents hosted a lot of social events, so by age five, I was already walking around at parties in my little sweater vest and tie, serving coffee, answering the doorbell, and making small talk with people I had just met. Also, my parents had an eclectic mix of friends and colleagues—Asian, Mexican, African-American, gay, you name it—and I think as a result of having been exposed to such a variety of people, I can interact with just about anyone. I think this had to do with why it was so easy for me to relax and have fun with everyone on *The Bachelorette*.

On the first night of taping, the bachelors all piled into limousines that would take us to a party at a palatial mansion, where we would first meet Trista. In my limo were Duane, a pilot instructor from Chicago City, Minnesota; Gregg H., a blue-eyed guy from New Jersey; Jack, a firefighter, whom everybody remembers as the guy who got drunk the second night and peed all over his bed; and Brian C., who looked like JFK Jr.—all the guys were really handsome, and we got along great. Brian and his twin brother ran a mortgage company, so we talked a lot about business during the ride.

We all wore designer suits. Unfortunately, I hated my suit because, of course, it had been tailored too tight. Jamie (one of the other bachelors, who has since become one of my best friends from the show) later joked that when I got out of the limo, one of my buttons popped off and hit him in the eye! It was pretty bad. I think what happened was that the tailor must have thought, *There's no way this guy could be these dimensions if he's coming on this show!* So he tailored it too small.

Right away, I met the rest of the guys, and the atmosphere was pretty comfortable. It was a little weird having the cameras around, but not as weird as I thought it was going to be. The camera operators were uncannily discreet, and it was easy to forget they were around, unless a camera was shoved in your face (which happened from time to time throughout the taping of the series). But that night's party felt pretty normal. As we sat around and talked, I realized that most of the other guys were there for the same reason I was—to have fun and to meet an amazing woman.

That first night, I wasn't even sure exactly why I was there. I was open to finding love, but the reality was that the pain of my divorce was still a bit fresh. I wasn't sure if I was ready to feel anything strong or true for anyone. But I was willing to experience everything and see where it might take me.

Trista was very beautiful, calm, and kind. We hit it off immediately, but I knew pretty early on that it was the kind of rapport that meant we were going to be friends to begin with, and then possibly go from there. Perhaps if we had had more time together it might have turned into something more. Who knows? I was in a position in my life where I was definitely going to be a slow burn when it came to anything involving my heart.

Over the course of the party, Trista knew I liked her, and I could tell that she liked me. I made her laugh, and we had some sort of connection. I found that rewarding in itself.

Of course, like everyone else, I was on my best behavior—at least for a little while. But after making polite conversation and having a few drinks, it struck me that the gathering was just a tad too sedate. *This is a party!* I thought, and that's when I decided to blow things up a little. I got up in front of the room and started singing Journey tunes. Trista then mentioned, a bit teasingly, that she had heard I was an amazing dancer. This is when I busted out into the Running Man and then a jig to make everyone laugh. What can I say? It was really fun, and that's when I recognized my strong connection with everyone there and discovered Trista's sense of humor. It was good.

At that first rose ceremony, I was the last guy to get a rose. It was totally nerve-wracking. I didn't even know how I felt about being there, or whether I even wanted a rose, until the moment I thought I wasn't going to get one. Then I knew for sure that I wanted one. It was just that simple principle that something becomes so much more attractive when you suddenly fear you can't have it. Plus, I wanted a chance to get to know Trista better.

The guys' house was a cross between a frat house and a luxury hotel. There was a hot tub, a pool, and a basketball court. There were five bedrooms, so we slept three to a room. Everyone had to deal with snoring and teeth grinding and deciding which drawer was whose—all the little issues that come up when you share a bedroom with strangers. The saving grace was that all the guys were as considerate as possible of one another.

We were always horsing around with one another. There was one guy, Rob, who had really cool, funky blond hair—kind of on the long side, and a little spiky around the edges. (We called it "Hollywood hair.") He'd spend half an hour or more in the bathroom, getting it perfect for Trista's arrival. Every once in a while he'd come out of the bathroom and one of the guys would pounce on him and mess his hair up, so he'd have to go back into the bathroom and spend another twenty minutes on it.

■

THERE WASN'T ONE guy who I looked at and thought, *He doesn't belong.* I thought they all belonged there. If anything, *I* was the one who didn't belong there. But surprisingly, I never felt that way when I was actually there. There was a lot of camaraderie among us, and we totally backed each other up. It wasn't like we were hoping the other guys would go down. Granted, there were a couple of guys who kept to themselves or who were more reserved than others. But in general, we all really hit it off. It made the whole experience so much better.

Right away Trista and a few guys went on a group date to Las Vegas. I was disappointed about not going because I love Vegas and I love gambling, but I also knew that if I went it would have been a train wreck, because I was so tired. I would have just been gambling and drinking and making a fool of myself. So it was just as well that I stayed home.

The moment Trista left with her first batch of guys, all hell broke loose. Jamie, who is usually such a Boy Scout, was running around in his briefs, pouring dog food all over himself.

Another night, Jack peed on his bed and then passed out. I don't know whose idea it was to carry Jack's bed—with him asleep in it—to the front lawn, but one of us suggested it, and then the rest just decided to go with the flow.

Jamie, Charlie, Jack, and I became instant friends. We were on the same wavelength in a lot of ways. One day Jamie and I were shooting hoops when Trista arrived to pick up the boys. All the other guys playing basketball ran off the court to greet her, but we just kept playing. Neither of us realized what we were supposed to do. I think Trista actually liked it, but I'm not sure. In retrospect, it was actually kind of rude that we didn't go up there to greet her. But obviously it worked out all right.

Jamie and I actually hung out quite a bit. We were paired on all the group dates together. We'd enter the room and Trista would say, "Oh my God, shocker! You two walking in together." We even ended up leaving the show on the same night.

Jamie is a handsome fellow with unnaturally white teeth. But what I didn't know at first was that he suffers from a debilitating panic disorder. I found it hard to believe that a person who presented himself as being so together could have such a problem. In fact, when he first told me about his disorder, I thought he was kidding. I didn't see any way at all that this guy could have any issues like that. I mean, he was a professional basketball player in Europe at one time. It really brought things into perspective for me.

In fact, a real eye-opener was getting to know the other guys on the show and realizing that they *all* had problems—it wasn't just me. I had assumed everyone in the house was perfect, except me—I felt like damaged goods. But spending time with the other guys helped me see that I had been comparing my insides to their outsides. After the filming of the show had started, I quickly began to feel better about myself. Making it through the first rose ceremony definitely helped—it was such a strong vote of confidence.

The guys' house was very similar to my frat house at college. We ordered in groceries, and Jack would do the cooking, since he was used to preparing meals as one of his duties at the firehouse. We didn't have a housecleaner, so things degenerated pretty quickly; we pushed old food to the back of the refrigerator to make room for the new, and there were always dirty dishes in the sink because we always forgot to order sponges and dish soap. I have to admit, though, that I'm a bit anal, and so I was constantly wiping up things. In fact, a lot of the guys did. But I think it's just natural for that many guys to forget how important it might be to clean up once in a while.

■

ONCE JACK LEFT the show, I took over some of the cooking responsibilities. I wasn't as accomplished a chef as Jack, so mostly we ate anything that I could throw on the grill—burgers and chicken and sausages. Guys would just come and grab what they wanted. Since I had been the social director at my frat, I immediately fell into the role of the house party planner. It's just my nature to take over things.

This had its drawbacks. I think Trista was a little surprised by how much we could party, and she figured out quickly that I was one of the ringleaders. How could she help but see the pattern? When she went out with me, she'd come home and all the guys would be relaxed or asleep. When she went out without me, she'd come home and everyone would be having a blast. I guess that was partly my doing.

I am a very private person, and at times, as I mentioned, I can be kind of anal, even though I don't always come across that way. I hadn't had a roommate since shortly after college, other than the brief period when my friend Weaz was living with me. So living with all these other guys became difficult at times because there was basically no privacy. But I did have a great time.

After a couple weeks, three of Trista's friends came for a visit. We hadn't seen a woman (besides Trista) in so long, so it was a refreshing change to have some around—they provided the female company that we desperately needed. They helped balance out the atmosphere of the home and make it less testosterone-based. I remembered Shannon from the first show, of course, and I particularly enjoyed talking with her. She was just as beautiful in person as she appeared to be on TV. The women were very generous about putting in time to teach us how to clean the refrigerator, and they helped get the house back into some semblance of order.

As the days went by and the rose ceremonies went on, everything seemed to be going fine. It wasn't until the night before the rose ceremony when I ended up getting cut that my fear of commitment emerged. I started wondering if it was time for me to go.

It all came to a head when we were hanging out and Greg T.,

the bachelor who was always playing his guitar, said, "Hey, isn't this weird? In a couple weeks, maybe one of us will be engaged to Trista."

I got a serious case of cold feet. At the next rose ceremony, I remember talking a lot about my family and how much I loved Detroit. I mentioned what a great life I had in Michigan, and we talked about a real relationship having compromises from both sides. I don't know why I felt it was *so* important to harp on that, but I did.

While I was scared about the prospect of things advancing so far with her, at the same time I was still open to all possibilities. I really liked Trista, and I wasn't willing to give up as long as there was a chance that she and I could possibly be a match. One part of me wanted to go home, but then another part of me didn't.

In the end, however, it wasn't my choice to make. At the next rose ceremony, I didn't get a rose, and that was that. But Trista was very sweet and kind to say that if she had had another rose, it would have been mine. I have a lot of respect for Trista. She's truly remarkable and has become a dear friend.

And she's very intuitive. I suspect that she must have picked up on the fact that I was still perhaps wounded from my divorce. I know that Trista felt we were a better friend match than a romantic one, and I agree with her. I don't think she would have chosen me as the one, even if our feelings had been romantically stronger for each other. She was looking for the right person, and it was so obvious that she and Ryan were head over heels for each other. All the guys saw it from the beginning. She's a smart woman—she made sure to choose someone who was crazy about her. I personally don't think it's a coincidence that of all the people who have gone on all the reality shows, she's been one who made a good match and has been able to make it stick, because she was looking for the right stuff. Other people have just picked the hottest person, but she went into the show with a different mind-set. Not that Ryan isn't a good-looking guy—he is. But he also has qualities that go much deeper. I've often said that anyone who would have seen them together and stood in the way of them getting together would have to be a complete jackass. And I've meant it.

I realize now that it was a big thing for me to know when it was time to get out. As you know by now, I've been prone to sticking around as long as possible, no matter what, with my eye on the prize. I realized that the prize would be too much for me to bear— I couldn't do it. It was a good time for me to go, and I went home.

All in all, it was a great experience, and I think it's a testament to the producers of the show that even though I was clearly not a supermodel type at the time, they still chose me. Looking back, I have to say I'm surprised that I was chosen. I wonder what they saw in me. But I'm very grateful that I had the opportunity. It helped me get my confidence back after it had been dealt such a blow.

On one episode of the show I said, "The everyman will always defeat the other guys." It's a statement I fully believe. There are a lot of people who look slick on paper, but then you meet them and they aren't everything you thought they would be. A guy can work hard and make a lot of money and have a gym-toned body, but if he has no personality or integrity, he isn't actually all that great. The total package is important, and sometimes the everyman has that package. In any event, this particular everyman left the show feeling a hell of a lot better about himself than he did when he arrived.

I went back to the house that Jennifer and I had once shared.

Although I'd been gone only a few weeks, it felt like a year. I had missed my neighborhood, which was kind of an alternative community—a mix of young, single people and young hetero and gay couples, which makes for a great community. My neighbors throw great parties and keep their houses and lawns in perfect shape. All my neighbors are very nice people. They kept an eye on my house when I was gone during filming, so I didn't have to worry while I was away.

It was good to get away and have such an amazing experience. And then it was so good to be home again.

■

IN THE BEGINNING, a lot of the hype about the show was that the woman would be proposing, but in the end it didn't work out that way. I think that any one of the bachelors would have wanted to propose instead of being proposed to. It probably taps into the same feelings that made me want my wife to take my last name. There are some things that you want to keep if you are traditional, and I'm an old-fashioned guy in a lot of ways, and so were a lot of the other guys there.

Jamie visited me after filming had stopped but before the show aired. It was funny—I hadn't told anyone I'd done the show. Jamie was shocked that a lot of the guys on the show didn't know that I had been in a band. He was shocked that most of them didn't know I owned a branch of a mortgage company or that I had been a football player in college.

He said, "Man, you are the most humble guy," and that was really flattering.

It was great to realize that the relationships I had made on the show were genuine, and that nothing had changed. It was especially nice to be able to keep in touch with a lot of the guys from the show after it was over. I often talk to Brook from Texas, Rob from Mississippi, Brian H. from Ohio, Russ from California, Ryan and Charlie, Jack and Jamie. We kept a pretty tight circle to make sure we all knew how everybody else was doing.

Once the filming was over and we were all home, the preshow publicity started, and all the bachelors were vulnerable to criticism. I received phone calls from friends and family who had gone online and read what people were saying in the chat rooms and on the message boards. I was kind of shocked. I was hurt that everyone was calling me fat. Now that I'm a little wiser, I know that if you're in the public eye, people are going to rip on you. But in the beginning I wasn't prepared for it, and I surprised myself by being so affected by these mean-spirited comments. It was funny because even though I was heavier than I'd been in previous years, I still wasn't *that* fat.

As it so happens, I have lost almost forty pounds since *The Bachelorette*. I'm back to my normal size. Regardless, I am exactly the same person I was when I was overweight, and I just don't understand what all the fuss was about. Whether you're fat or slender doesn't have anything to do with whether or not you're a good person.

Somebody said to me recently, "You can't do the fat jokes anymore. You're not fat," and I said, "Thanks for noticing." I never meant to offend anyone, but I'll make any jokes that I damn well please.

10.

■

NOVEMBER

Learn not to measure yourself by how you look on paper,
but by who you know you are.

A FTER THE SHOW I was back at the same house, the same
job, and the same routine, and on one hand, I felt like I
hadn't changed a bit—but on the other, I felt like I had changed a
lot. It was very difficult, because I'd had the extraordinary experience of being on a TV show, but I couldn't share it with anyone.
Nevertheless, I never came close to spilling the beans or compro-
mising my confidentiality agreement, even though my friends and
family kept trying to get me to spill. (I'm a good person to confide
in, because I try to take my secrets to the grave.)

I sent a lot of thank-you cards when I got home. I sent one to
Trista, telling her how much fun I'd had and how I wished her the
best, and then she called me, and we started a genuine friendship.

I didn't know what was happening on the show after I left—the
bachelors didn't get any insider information once we'd been given

the boot—but I was certainly curious. I had the definite feeling she was going to pick Ryan. In fact, I couldn't imagine she would choose anyone else. Even though since leaving the show I've kept in better contact with Charlie than with Ryan, I really thought she *should* pick Ryan—it was so plain to everyone how much he genuinely cared for her. When we were at the guys' house, he had moments when he would get very reflective when he talked about Trista. It was clear from the look he'd get on his face that he was in love. The rest of us guys would be playing pool or swimming, and he'd go off to his room and compose poetry for her. When a guy is off writing love poetry instead of hanging with the gang, he usually becomes the target of some pretty serious grief, but we didn't tease Ryan, because it was all so heartfelt. We respected what he was feeling. I think that says a lot about the maturity of the men in the house.

■

SINCE I'D SPENT the past few weeks having the time of my life, once I was off the show I had to shift gears and get back to work. I transitioned myself from Shangri-la in Southern California to the workaday life in the Midwest by taking the long way home. I reacclimated by spending the weekend with friends in San Diego, which kind of eased me back into the real world.

Greg had been great about keeping my end of the business running smoothly while I was gone, and my staff had helped a lot, too. It was tricky because we didn't know how long I was going to be away or when I would be back. And since I was sequestered, they hadn't had much contact with me.

Still, there was a lot of catching up for me to do—a huge stack of papers on my desk and a thousand e-mail messages to return. Once I was behind my desk, I got right back into the mind-set of trying to make headway in my business. I put the world of rose ceremonies and hot tubs behind me, and I threw myself into the world of interest rates and bank loans.

Some of my clients said, "Where have you been for the past six weeks?" And I just said that I was in California on business, and it wasn't a lie; I *had* been away on business—business of the heart and the mind.

That winter, when I needed a break from my work, I'd go up to the cottage and hang with friends. Although it's cold in Northeast Michigan in the late fall, it's not as cold as you might think. A wind comes off the lake, but it's not an arctic blast. I love the crispness. There's a big fireplace in the cottage, and when I was a kid, the fireplace was our only source of heat in the winter. Now we have central heating, but there's nothing more fun than kicking back in front of a fire. I'm less of a fan of Michigan winters now, only because of the fact that I can no longer do everything I used to love to do in the winter. I have more knee surgeries under my belt than I care to mention, so it makes me hesitate to strap on the boards and hit the slopes. But the winters are truly beautiful.

Thanksgiving that year was bittersweet. It was nearing the first anniversary of Jennifer leaving, but it was also the first time in a long while that I could devote all my attention to my family. We all gathered at Dee Dee's house. J.D. is an outstanding and adventurous cook, so although we had the standard roast turkey, he threw in some nontraditional dishes that were killer, like roasted eggplant and his delightful spicy sausage stuffing. My job was to bartend and stay out of the way of the people in the kitchen.

"Go on, Bob, tell us about the show," my mother said over dinner. "You've been silent too long."

"What show?" I asked, spooning gravy and cranberry sauce over my turkey.

"You know exactly what we're talking about," said J.D. "Were you the one she picked? Or were you the runner-up?"

"I'm sorry, but I just can't say," I told them. "I've been sworn to secrecy."

Later, as I loaded dishes into the dishwasher, Dee Dee sidled up to me.

"But you're going to tell me, right?" she whispered.

I smiled. "Sorry."

"But you know that I can really keep a secret," she protested. I didn't reply, and after a moment, it sunk in.

"You mean you're *really* not going to tell me?" she asked.

"That's right. You'll have to wait to see it on prime time, like everybody else."

She gasped in mock fury and hit me with the dish towel.

■

ONE DAY IN NOVEMBER, something really big hit me. I was thinking about how on paper I looked to myself like someone who'd been less successful than he planned at everything he did. My friends and family would argue against this statement—but I was a tougher critic. After all, my early promise as an athlete had come to nothing, my music career hadn't gone anywhere, and my marriage had fallen apart after only two years. But the reality of where I was at that point—the part of me that you couldn't see from the outside—was that I was actually doing great. I had worked hard to build up a successful business, I had made some fundamental changes that led to a much healthier relationship with my family and friends and with myself, and I had just taken part in an amazing experience that was about to air nationally. I wasn't a loser at all. In fact, professionally and emotionally speaking, I was in the best place I'd ever been in my life.

Sadly, in this culture I think we're taught to judge people by the outer trappings—what kind of car they drive, or what kind of job they have. I realized that that's exactly what I'd been doing—but I had been judging myself. And you can't assess yourself by external markers. You have to judge yourself by who you know you are. And I knew that I was somebody who had tried to stay human in difficult situations, and it had paid off.

The more I got myself out there, the more people I met, and the more I made myself open to new experiences, the better I felt. I was enormously proud that I hadn't let a crisis in my life destroy me. I had battled tooth and nail to get back to this place where I could feel good about myself again. And it was ironic that even though I no longer bought completely into the whole "winners never quit, and quitters never win" mentality, there was still a tiny part of me that believed that things would always work out if you aren't ever willing to give up.

11.

◼

DECEMBER

We're all given the same opportunities and chances to do things.
The difference is how much we are prepared to run with them.

UNCLE BIG RED

M Y UNCLE BIG RED'S real name was Lucious Adolphus Sandifer, named after his father, whom everyone called "Doc." Uncle Big Red was my mom's brother, and he was a real piece of work. He had been a football superstar—a star tailback in high school, and then an offensive lineman in college. His philosophy in life was, "Keep your feet square and your head up, hit through the body—mass plus velocity equals pain," or something like that. I thought it was genius.

He used to say the funniest things. Once, at an MSU football game, he had been a little "overserved" with his crew of buddies and asked me to drive him home in his town car. I was all of about fourteen. About a half-mile to his house, he said, "Bobby, you gotta pull over, 'cause I've got to piss like a six-dick billy goat." He was honestly one of the coolest people I have ever known.

Uncle Big Red also said some serious things that have stuck with me to this day. He believed that it isn't how many chances you get but what you do with the ones that come to you.

He also believed in being prepared. You can prepare yourself for the opportunities that come your way, or you can go around with your head in the clouds only to find out that—*Bam!*—opportunity is knocking but you don't know what to do about it because you're not ready to go for it.

When it comes to sports, being fully prepared is both a physical and a mental thing. My sophomore year of high school, my coach didn't tell me I was going to be the starting quarterback of the opening season game until the day of the game, because he didn't want me to get nervous. Well, I got nervous anyway. I was ready physically but not mentally—I fumbled the ball. I had to reframe the moment so that it became just another game and not the biggest possible choke moment of my lifetime. Then I was able to start playing to win instead of playing not to lose.

I kept my Uncle Big Red's attitude about opportunity very much in mind when I went on *The Bachelorette*. I really made a conscious decision that I was going to make the most of it. I decided to use it as a chance to have a great experience. I decided to have as much fun as I could, and I think the other guys picked up on that right away. In the end, I really do think I've come out the big winner. Many of the other guys and the producers are now my friends. So are Trista and Ryan. As a matter of fact, they have invited me to attend their wedding and have even asked me to sing at the event.

By December, my Achilles tendon was almost completely back to normal, and I started working out and playing sports again. I ran at the gym every morning and played basketball at night. The fact was, I had gotten used to myself with the extra weight and accepted my body for what it was. My goal wasn't to get six-pack abs or grapefruit-sized biceps; I just wanted to be healthier, and I was enjoying the activity that I hadn't been able to indulge in for more than a year. Nevertheless, the weight melted off, and I ended up losing about forty pounds. I changed my diet a little bit and exercised a lot more—but I wasn't fanatical. It took about six to seven months to get back to the normal me and to wear some of my favorite clothes again without looking like a freak. I felt so much better.

■

THE HOLIDAYS WERE different for me that year because I wasn't still trying to convince everyone that I was still part of a happy couple. Now I could just be myself, and it was certainly easier not to have to run all over the place trying to please two families all the time.

But it wasn't all easy. Holidays are a family time, and since Jennifer had been part of my family for so long, and I a part of hers, I missed her and thought about her, but I was certainly better off than I had been the year before.

On Christmas morning, I was at my sister's house early. In my family, if you're not there Christmas morning, opening gifts, you aren't really part of the true experience. It was particularly fun because my sister's son, Jack, was at the perfect age—old enough to really understand and enjoy what was happening, but not old enough to be jaded, thinking about the gifts alone. It was really special to see the look of joy and astonishment in his eyes when he came out in the morning and saw the overstuffed stockings and the gifts set up around the tree. My family does Christmas like a circus. It's nuts! He came out and all the toys were running, even a train going around the tree. It really captured the excitement of Christmas morning for a child, I think.

He's a very appreciative kid—not at all the "me, me, me" type. He was so thankful for every gift he got. And then while he was opening his gifts, he gave me one to hold so I wouldn't feel left out.

Later that afternoon, more relatives came over. They rushed over to me without taking off their coats and crushed me with their hugs. No one went out of their way to mention Jennifer or the divorce, or the fact that she wasn't there. They just said how happy they were to have me there for the whole day. I had the chance to have a long talk with my family that night, and I tried to express to each of them how much I loved and cared for them. The whole crew was there from my mom's side of the family, and it was a very special Christmas for me.

Previews of *The Bachelorette* started appearing after Christmas, a few weeks before the show aired. I had told almost no one that I had done the show, other than my family and a couple close friends, so all of a sudden my phone started ringing off the hook with people saying, "I just saw you on an ad for a reality show!" People who knew me were really shocked.

There was, however, a downside. When the preview aired, everyone started slamming me on the Internet chat boards, calling me fat and asking, "What the hell is this guy doing here?" I was already a whole new person physically, but those comments still hurt. The first show hadn't even aired yet, and I was already getting nonstop criticism.

I began to wonder what I had gotten myself into, and I really got worried about the series airing. Was I going to be publicly trashed? Would I become some kind of national laughingstock? I went through a period of really wondering why I had set myself up for such abuse.

And I was so surprised by how strongly some people reacted to my being a bit overweight at the time. It puzzled me because I knew that some of these people were on the Internet all day long, so I had the suspicion that more than a few of them were probably carrying a couple of extra pounds themselves—unless their keyboards were duct-taped to their treadmills.

They also came down hard on me for being divorced. They'd say, "How much of a catch can he be if he's divorced?" But this was kind of hypocritical, too—statistically speaking, more than half of all new marriages end in divorce. It's a sad statistic, and I couldn't help but wonder if the people on the message boards trashing me hadn't gone through it too. Of course I heard about a lot of people saying very nice things as well, but strangely, when it was happening to me, I focused only on the bad stuff. The ego is a tough thing to cope with sometimes.

Since then, I have come to understand that much of this kind of reaction is based on the unfortunate feeling of self-recognition that people sometimes have when they look at another person. Fans project a lot when it comes to reality shows because the cast members are normal people, not celebrities. But at the time I didn't understand that what they were saying was as much about themselves as it was about me. It all seemed unfair, and I wondered what kind of nightmare experience might be in store for me when the show started airing.

12.

■

JANUARY

When you're really honest about who you are,
people will be drawn to you.

I HAVE NEVER really enjoyed New Year's Eve. It seems like one of those holidays that never lives up to the hype. But I did celebrate it on this particular year—in fact, I actually threw my own party. My sister and brother-in-law went shopping and prepared a bunch of party platters and did a lot of cooking, and I bought a couple cases of champagne. We had about fifty guests, all of them dressed up and ready to ring in the new year.

I cringed as I remembered how horrible the last New Year's Eve had been—when I ran around, looking for Jennifer to get our midnight kiss—but I actually felt hopeful about going into the next year. For several months, I had done what was good for me instead of what other people wanted, and it had gone so well that my New Year's resolution was to keep going with this way of thinking. Remarkably, I've really stuck to that resolution.

As soon as the new year began, the airing of the first episode was right around the corner. I tried to tell myself that whatever was going to happen was out of my hands. I had been myself on the show, and that was the important thing. I've never tried to pretend I'm something I'm not. It isn't hard for me to act natural, because who I am at heart has been pretty much unchanged since I was a kid. I'm not a complicated person. I have never taken myself too seriously, and that's the way I was on the show.

A week before the first show aired, I thought I'd better give Jennifer a heads-up. I left her a message letting her know we needed to talk. Soon after, she showed up at my house. It was awkward to tell her at first. She's a very private person, and so naturally she was concerned about how my being on national TV might affect her, and I respected that. But I hadn't made her look bad on the show, or talked about our personal life. It took a little time to convince her of that.

Eventually, she understood that I was just trying to move on, to feel better about myself, and to have an experience out of the norm to shake things up and get back on track. She came to accept that it didn't have anything to do with her—or us. It was all about me and my trying to get past our divorce. She had moved on by dating another man; I had moved on by going on national television. Similar, but so different!

Besides, I had the newfound attitude that I just couldn't please everyone, and this was a situation in which somebody I cared about was not going to be pleased. It was an important step for the new me. At the same time, I felt she deserved to know about the show and to hear it from me.

The first episode of *The Bachelorette* aired January 8. I had a party at my house, with thirty-five to forty people. ABC sent out a crew to film the party and interview my guests. Once I saw the first episode, I knew I was going to be fine. I was so impressed by how the producers had put it together, and I loved the way they showed that we had all been friends, instead of trying to make us look as if we were competitive, when we weren't.

After the series had started to air, the message boards became overwhelmingly positive. I suddenly had a legion of fans. It was amazing. To my surprise, I quickly became one of the favorites from the show. It was the last thing I had expected, and it gave me a huge shot of self-esteem. I had been myself on camera, so I knew that people were reacting to the true me.

Needless to say, my friends, my parents, and my brother-in-law and sister (and my whole family, in fact) thought my whole *Bachelorette* experience was a complete riot. In particular, they thought it was really funny that people couldn't believe that how I was on the show is exactly how I am at home. Of course, my family and friends see it every day.

When people who have watched the show meet me in person for the first time, they usually say, "Wow, I never thought you'd be this nice." I never know how to respond to this. I am who I am, and I don't pretend to be anything else. Let's face it, I was on a reality TV show—I'm not George Clooney.

As for all the remarks about my weight on the show—I take all responsibility. I made sure I joked about it first before anyone else had a chance to. And I thought the show really presented us as we were and was terrific. I would call the producers after every show to tell them how much I liked it. They made me come across as really having fun instead of as a buffoon—either of which would have been completely possible.

I chose to watch many of the rest of the episodes with just my family and friends, and not to do it publicly. It became a tradition to have "*Bachelorette* parties," and we would switch houses every week and watch the show together. As the show progressed, I got as caught up in it and was just as eager to see the outcome as the rest of the nation.

The funny thing was that most of my friends and family still didn't know at this point whether or not I was the guy she had picked. And I loved faking them out and hinting that I was. I would leave Trista a message and if she happened to call me back while I was with friends or family, they'd see "Trista Rehn" on the caller ID on my cell phone and be like, "Oh, my god! It's true! You two are an item!" It was hilarious.

During that month, I didn't know if Jennifer was watching *The Bachelorette* or what her thoughts were about it. We never discussed it. But I was sure that it had to be difficult to watch, knowing that everyone was referring to her ex-husband as "Bachelor Bob." She did mention to me more than once that she had seen me on television a few times. It was nice that she was watching some of the shows, but I wouldn't have blamed her if it all felt a little overwhelming. The universe was rewarding me in some pretty fantastic ways, and as much as you may care for someone, post-divorce it's hard to revel in their bachelordom.

For some reason, whenever I think of my time with Jennifer, my mind always goes back to a day when she and I felt so close. Jennifer was not a performer—that was always my thing—but once she decided she wanted to be in the musical *Grease* at a local theater.

I was so proud that she was willing to try something so different and unusual for her. Amid all the turmoil that she and I had been through over the last few years, this was one event that stood out as a time when we grew so much closer. She actually had a really good singing voice—we worked on it together. She was already a great dancer (she'd been a national champion dancer in high school). Unfortunately, despite all the hard work she did preparing, she didn't get into the play. We were both sad, but I was still so happy she'd taken a shot at it. I'm not sure that I would have had the guts to do the same.

■

ONE DAY IN JANUARY, Jennifer called to discuss a joint bank account that we had never closed. Then she said, "Your face is splashed all over the place. I can't turn around without seeing an image of you."

"I know," I said. "It's weird, isn't it? Who would have imagined?"

She sighed and said, "It's kind of odd because I know that if we hadn't divorced, none of this would have ever happened." I knew how difficult all this must have been for Jennifer to deal with. I honestly hadn't thought much about it before then.

I told her, "You know, Jennifer, I've been lucky, but what have I really done? I would trade it all to be in a good marriage with you."

She didn't reply. We both knew that the time when that would have been possible had long passed for us. I finally realized that our lives would most likely be separate from that point forward.

The thing about the opportunities I've had is that I hadn't expected any of them—I hadn't expected anything more to come from my appearance on the show. But to my surprise, after the episode when I got tossed off, the opportunities grew for me. I had a spot on *Good Morning America, Connie Chung,* and *Fox News Live.* I sang on *The Wayne Brady Show* and *The Caroline Rhea Show.* I met with E! and VH1. Then it all escalated from there. All of a sudden, I was being approached to host shows and comedy events, and suddenly record labels were getting in touch. I kept thinking that things were going to mellow out, but they never did. Speaking tours and TV commercials and radio interviews—everything was being thrown my way. And it still is.

Although I enjoy going on TV and I really liked all the people I met on the shows, I have to say that some tended to ask the same questions over and over. I got *really* sick of watching the clip of me doing the Running Man. By the end, I felt like if I watched it one more time I was going to have to gouge my eyes out. Please, I'm begging—let's put Running Man to rest once and for all. Maybe we can bring back The Robot.

13.

◼

FEBRUARY

When you work your way through a crisis and fight hard to make a full recovery, you come out of the experience a stronger, better person.

WHO WOULD HAVE known I would win so much by losing? By the anniversary of my discovering the sticky note, my life had been transformed. I was comfortable financially through my work, I was having a blast on the dating scene, and I was a new—if somewhat unlikely—"pseudo celebrity." And no one was more astonished than I was.

One day, my phone rang. A voice from the past was on the other end of the line—my ex-therapist, John.

"I caught you on *The Bachelorette* last night," he said. "I couldn't believe how happy and well adjusted you look! It's really remarkable."

Just hearing John's voice made me remember the first few times I went to see him. I was still with Jennifer—unhappy, but not understanding how unhappy I really was. And then I thought about the sessions when I had sat on his couch, flattened by pain.

Now I felt like a man who had climbed a mountain and who can look behind him and understand how much distance he had covered, and what it all meant.

"Can you believe how far I've come?" I asked him, feeling a swell of pride.

"Well, you must have had a good counselor," he said, and we laughed together.

"The best," I agreed.

The Bachelorette reunion show aired in February. By that time, I was being referred to by some as the "funny" bachelor. A sweetheart! Who would have dreamed? Not me. At the reunion show, the crowd went wild when they called my name. Afterward, I had to go into the audience and sign autographs and shake hands and kiss babies, so to speak. One thing I have been grateful for is that I have had all this attention and all these opportunities, and none of my friends from the show have been weird or negative about it. Of course, they get a ton of it, too.

Then one day an ABC publicist called and said, "Are you sitting down?"

I said, "No, I'm standing up," and she said, "Well, you might want to sit down, because Oprah wants to have you on her show." I was totally floored. It turned out that I was the first person from reality TV that she had invited on. It was going to be a show about three married guys who didn't know how to cook, and then me, the bachelor who didn't know how, either. It was going to air on Valentine's Day.

My mom is a huge Oprah fan. So is Dee Dee. When they found out that I was going to be on the show, they went nuts. My mother actually cried. The show was so much fun to do. (Unfortunately, I still can't cook.)

Since then, I've been on *The Oprah Winfrey Show* several more times. I've been asked to speak all over the country on all different kinds of topics. The most rewarding engagement was speaking at my old college, to my favorite communications class, with my favorite professor, Steven McCornack, who asked me to talk about interpersonal relationships and media relations.

I spoke at my high school's Honor Society induction, too. I loved that because I wasn't even in the National Honor Society! (At the time, you needed a 3.5, and I had only a 3.0.) The only bad part about that speech was that my favorite teacher from high school, Mr. Paul Menard, was not in attendance. And that was half the reason I wanted to do it.

It's funny, because those small going-back-home talks flatter me sometimes just as much, if not more, than being on the national TV shows. They're hilariously fun. I love the chance to give back a bit. And I love seeing my old school and the teachers.

What I perhaps love most is when the public attention reflects on my family. For example, one day I was in South Carolina with my Uncle Clyde (my Grandma Sandifer's brother), who has always been an inspiration for me as an athlete. He was a collegiate All-American for the University of South Carolina, and then he played pro football for the Ottawa Roughriders. Afterward, he earned the Purple Heart multiple times in Vietnam. When we were in South Carolina recently, a man and woman approached me and told me that I was the inspiration for the man to get himself in shape, and for them both to work on their relationship. My Uncle

Clyde was so impressed—which made me feel great, as I felt he deserved part of the credit.

People often ask my friends how all this media attention has changed me, and I've heard them say it hasn't changed me at all—and that's a huge compliment. It has changed me—I'm only human—but it hasn't affected my relationships with the people I really care about or the way that I interact with them.

Years ago I learned an important lesson about handling success from my high school football coach, Donald G. Lessner (whom we players called Bluker, or "The Duke of Darkness"). At a crucial moment in that first game, after fumbling the ball, I got it together and scored my first touchdown. I was so excited, I started pumping my fist in the air. After the game, the coach played the footage over and over. He played it probably a hundred times, making me look like a total idiot. Then he said, "Hey, Guiney, do me a favor. Next time, make it look like you've been there before." He taught us to be gracious in victory as well as in defeat. So no matter how many great opportunities may come my way in the future, I'll try to take it in stride and act like I've been there before. I try to be as appreciative as I can for the opportunities. No one deserves anything in life—it's all gravy.

■

BY THE END of February, my life had gotten pretty hectic. I was trying to balance all the publicity and speaking engagements with my mortgage business. But I wasn't going to abandon the business I had built up for my fifteen minutes of fame. I would never do that to Greg. Sometimes I wished all of this hoopla had started before I started the business. At the same time, I felt I was lucky—if I

hadn't been my own boss, I would have been working for someone else and I probably would have lost my job for being gone so
much. I was very fortunate to have had the freedom to come
and go.

Besides, as I said earlier, Greg has shouldered a heavy burden
without complaining, but I think that just speaks to his character
and his dedication to me as a friend.

As for Beeba and Janaya, they couldn't believe everything that
had happened as a result of their going on the *Bachelorette* website.
Sometimes I think they wish they hadn't done it! For one thing,
my life has become so busy, and they've had to pick up a lot of my
slack. But I think they've been happy for me and proud of what
they made happen.

Still, their efforts had ultimately come to naught, because I
came out of the experience still a bachelor, in every sense of the
word. I wasn't ready to get hitched again, not yet. But I *wanted* to
be ready, and I believed that was half the battle. I knew that someday I wanted to meet the right woman, be married, and have a
family. As always, I was still optimistic. I can look back with the
wisdom that only time can bring. I know now that the suffering I
went through is going to make me a better husband to the future
Mrs. Guiney, because I know that I can do better in my next relationship. I have higher standards about what I want in return. Like
Claudia said, I want to be someone's favorite thing to do. I want a
better-than-best friend. I want a person who just can't wait to tell
me when something great happens. Or when something bad happens. I want to be with someone who gets excited by what I do
and what I have to say. Someone who can see the beauty and the
humor in life. Someone who can get emotional over stupid things,

like television commercials or movies that make you cry. And I want to give this all back—and more—in return.

My favorite movie is *It's a Wonderful Life*. I watch it every Christmas, and I cry like a baby. It's a tradition at my house. I just bawl until I can't even stand myself. I'm so deeply touched by that film because I think it's the classic story of the guy who has always tried to do the right thing, and in the end, he understands how much he's been rewarded for it. I want someone who doesn't mind getting messy with me over a film like that.

But she also needs to understand that I love the movie *Goodfellas,* too. Not quite the same type of movie, but a damn fine film. I'm not *all* sap.

■

BY FEBRUARY I was living in the public eye, and that was incredibly different and often tough to manage. When I first embarked on this long journey, I didn't think about what it was going to be like to be a "pseudo celebrity," because I didn't expect to be one. I was taken by surprise by what media attention was actually like. If a friend of mine was deciding whether or not to do something that would put him in this position, I'd tell him to consider it very, very carefully. It's fun, it's a rush, but it's also a lot of work at times.

I had been a regular guy who went about his business like anyone else. Now, when I went out in public, I couldn't have a conversation without people just coming up to talk to me or asking to have their picture taken with me. Not that I complained. It would have been worse if no one had paid attention to me at all. It is a small price I had to pay for all the wonderful things that have happened. In fact, recently a man said something hilarious to me:

"Hey, if you don't want to talk to somebody, don't leave your house!" It was an excellent point, and very well taken.

Oprah said it best one day: Any form of celebrity—whether real or pseudo—inherently brings with it a responsibility. I'm thankful for the fact that people relate to me, and I know it's not easy to approach a stranger, celebrity or not. As long as this bubble lasts for me, I will take the responsibility of being appreciative very seriously.

I used to read about celebrities complaining about media attention and wonder, *What are those people complaining about?* Now, of course, I have a new understanding; I have only a fraction of the celebrity status that they do, and yet my life has changed so much. I can only imagine what a *real* celebrity has to deal with.

Also, I used to be someone who always took what I read at face value. But after reading a ton of stuff about my ex-wife and myself in the tabloids that was so untrue, I know firsthand that you just can't believe everything you read. And when it comes to the tabloids, what you read will most likely not be flattering. They're not usually out to make you look good. I have learned that you have to have a good sense of self so that you don't get too bruised when you get beaten up by the press. And even with a good sense of self, you can still get bruised. So you better make sure you have a good sense of humor, too.

After *The Bachelorette* aired, I quickly became the poster boy for self-deprecating humor. I've always made fun of myself. It's just the way that I am. I tend to joke about things other people probably wouldn't, because I'm just not that sensitive about them.

The thing I became known for joking about on the show was my weight. It didn't take me that long after the show to get back to my normal weight, but the issue lived on, becoming such a big deal in ways that I never expected. I actually experienced a bit of backlash from some overweight people, especially people who are heavier than I was when I was making all the fat jokes. But of course hurting anybody was never my intention. I didn't mean any disrespect toward anyone else, overweight or not. But whether I liked it or not, it had become my painful claim to fame. That and the damn Running Man. Everywhere I went, people would say things like, "Oh my God, you're not *that* fat in person" or "You're so much cuter in person." I appreciate the compliments—but they can be tough to hear at times.

And it really surprised me to learn that some people think that if you use self-deprecating humor, you're masking insecurities. I thought that was ridiculous. I had insecurities—we all do. But to say that my humor was trying to hide those things was absurd— I've always joked about the things that I was most comfortable with. I believed that if you could go through a really bad experience and come through it with your sense of humor still intact, you'd be smelling if not like a rose then at least like some variety of garden flower. Besides, I know I can take a joke.

I was also surprised by how critical some people can be. Maybe I was just extra-sensitive, because I myself had learned to be less judgmental about people since my divorce. Once you've hit rock bottom, you realize that anything can happen to anyone. It doesn't matter if you're a CEO or a garbage collector. Life can change in an instant. So I had really come to understand in a new way that I could never look at other people as being beneath me—or look at myself as being beneath them.

People have said that when it comes to reality TV, with all the supermodel types of participants, I didn't fit the mold. But how many of us really fit the mold in the first place? Not most of the people that I know. So in the end it felt good to have brought a little Midwestern reality—and specifically, a dose of Detroit flavor—to the Hollywood scene.

■

As I AM nearing the end of this book, I have to admit that at times I've felt self-conscious writing about myself when so much is going on in the world. Of course, on September 11, 2001, the entire nation was stunned and saddened by what happened in our country. When the bombing occurred, I was still married and had no idea that I wouldn't be married in six months. My wife was supposed to fly out to New York on the following weekend. She had just started a clothing-design company, and she was going to New York to show her line. But after the disaster, they canceled the show. I remember thinking, *I know that Jennifer and I have problems, and I know I need to work on them, and I'm going to get started right now. There is no guarantee for tomorrow.* It made me understand how quickly things can change and how quickly things can be taken away from you. Then, five months later, everything did change for me and everything was taken away, in a totally different way.

And there have been many other important things going on in the world since 9/11, like the war in Iraq, where so many Americans had to worry about their loved ones who were in combat. So I have felt like people have had a lot more important things to think about lately than the life of one of the twenty-five guys from *The Bachelorette.*

Still, the turn of events in my life over the course of one year has been pretty incredible to me. Never in a million years would I have imagined that I'd be meeting Oprah Winfrey and Diane Sawyer and Connie Chung (not to mention Vince Neil of Mötley Crüe!), or that I'd be invited to the Academy Awards as a correspondent for *Extra*. As far as I'm concerned, that's about as exciting as it gets. But I didn't think these experiences would be of much interest to anyone else.

Then one day in February, I was in New York, at La Guardia Airport on my way back to Detroit. I had done several shows that day, and I was really tired. I was coming through security when a woman came up to me and said, "I'm sorry you didn't get a rose. You were great on the show and you made it so much fun. You had a lot of presence." She wished me luck, and I thanked her. Sometimes, after a long day like that one, when someone comes up to me in a public place, I'm not overly eager to chat, but she seemed really nice, and I was glad she'd stopped to say hello.

When I got onto my plane, it turned out that the woman I'd spoken to was sitting in the row behind me. We struck up a conversation—you know, the whole stranger-on-the-airplane thing, when you feel compelled to tell private things about yourself. I told her that after filming the reunion show, I had realized it was almost a year to the day that I'd come home to the biggest and most devastating disaster of my life, and here I was on top of the world. I just couldn't believe the wild and unpredictable turns my life had taken.

After we had been talking for a while, she took a business card out of her purse and handed it to me. It turned out that she was an editor at the Penguin Group. "If you want to do a book about your last year, give me a call," she said. I called her the next day. Before

I knew it, I had a book deal. It was yet one more unbelievable turn of events.

■

As for that famous sticky note, I never threw it away. I put it in a place of safekeeping. And as a result of writing this book, and all the old memories and emotions that it has stirred up, I recently got it back out and looked at it. I was really surprised to see that I had been wrong about a couple things. First, Jennifer didn't sign her name "J." She signed it "Jennifer." Second, there was something else on the note besides her statement that she wanted a divorce. She also wrote "I love you."

I guess that when your life is falling apart, all the painful and horrible stuff gets magnified so you can only remember the worst— in the middle of the nightmare that was unfolding, I just couldn't hear those three words from her.

But then when time has passed and the wounds have healed, you can go back and have another look at what happened. And sometimes what you find out is that the events from your past weren't quite as terrible as you remembered. And that's a great gift. You know that you're ready to move on when you've made peace with your past. Then, and only then, are you ready and able to move ahead to all the good things that are waiting for you. And *that's* the difference a year makes.

AFTERWORD

■ ■

From *The Bachelorette*
to *The Bachelor*

W HEN I FIRST got the offer to write this book, I didn't
know I was going to be the main man of the next *The
Bachelor*. Actually, when the producers called me and told me ABC
wanted me to be the next bachelor, I just laughed and said, "I don't
think so."

They didn't think it was funny. "Why aren't you jumping up and
down with excitement?"

"My days of reality TV are over," I told them, although even as
I said it I suspected they weren't. But the truth was, the reason I
didn't want to do the show was because I was scared. It seemed as
if there would be so much pressure on me to propose to one of the
women at the end. Even though I've had time to heal from my divorce, I didn't know when—if ever—I would be ready to commit
to marrying someone again. I had been down that road before, and

it had all gone wrong. I didn't want to make the same mistake twice. If I get married again, it'll have to be for keeps, and that's an extra pressure.

But after a while, I actually started to consider doing the show. It occurred to me that finding love the conventional way hadn't worked for me, so why not try the unconventional? I started talking about it with the people I love and trust. Honestly, I wrestled with the idea as if it were the biggest decision of my life—and that's because I think it *was* one of the biggest decisions I had in front of me. I knew it was going to require a commitment that I would have to take very seriously.

After giving it a lot of thought, I realized that the experience of my divorce was making me put too much pressure on the ending of the show. But there would also be the chance to have fun and meet women who might have seen the show and already liked me. They wouldn't come expecting someone else—or the unexpected—and that would make it a whole lot more real. However, I was still unsure. Maybe this was actually something else. Maybe I was being given a second chance in my life to do things differently. Maybe I was in the spot that would enable me to "play to win" in life and love, and not "play not to lose," like I had been guilty of before. I know it sounds like I was going a little overboard, considering it's "only" a dating show—believe me, I know. But it was a bigger thing to me than that. It was a challenge I wanted to meet.

What finally convinced me to do the show was a conversation I had with someone whom I love and care about. She told me that if I thought it out with my heart—and followed my heart—that everything would work out fine. If I thought too much with my head, I'd ruin it. And I knew she was right. She also said, "Enough of the hot tubs every five minutes. We're all sick of that!" I thought that was the funniest thing I'd ever heard. So I passed it on to ABC.

Also, I have made it clear to them that I am not guaranteeing anything—but I am open and hopeful for everything. Other people have made the promise of a proposal, and it has backfired. They promised the world and then failed to deliver, and that's not anything that I want to be a part of. I take proposing to someone very seriously. I'm not going to compromise my core beliefs for the sake of a TV show—or for anything, for that matter. But I will take it very seriously, as I know I'm dealing with people's emotions. And I really am open to wherever my feelings take me.

So if a young woman comes on the show, and she's nice and friendly—she'll come away with twenty-five new friends, including me. Bare minimum.

Who knows? I'm going into it with an honest and open heart, ready to see what happens. If nothing else, it's bound to be a valuable learning experience, just like every other thing that's happened to me over the past year or so.

But if Miss Right does turn up on the show, I will be open to the possibility of getting married again. I do think I could make someone a great husband. I'll make a better husband than I did the first time, because of how much the divorce forced me to learn about myself.

I used to tell people to marry their best friend—I did. But now I realize you need to marry someone who is better than your best friend. I already have a ton of best friends—I don't need another one. I'm looking for a woman I can trust with everything, someone I can talk to about anything, with the peace of knowing that she will not judge me, nor will I judge her. Someone to grow old with—who I know will really listen to what I have to say. Someone who'll do her best to understand me. And someone who I'll allow myself to understand.

In return, I'll give her total honesty, because I've come to understand how important that is. I'll keep everything out in the open, and I will be completely committed to her. The next time I walk down that aisle, I will be prepared to give my all to the marriage. If I'm lucky enough to marry again, my future wife is going to get a better deal than the first one did. I owe my ex-wife for all the things she forced me to understand that I never would have otherwise.

So I will go into the show with the attitude that if I meet the right woman, great. If I don't, that's okay, too. I wouldn't see coming away from the show still a bachelor as failure, because I have come to see that so many of the things I used to consider failings have turned out to be excellent learning experiences.

These experiences have also taught me more than just lessons in love. They've taught me a lot about people. Strangers have found me on several occasions since I was on *The Bachelorette*. One day, I was home and my doorbell rang. When I opened my door I found a group of women standing there. They told me that they had been sent on a treasure hunt—and I was the grand prize! There were seven of them, and they had rented a big white van and traveled all the way from Chicago, which is about a five-hour drive. I couldn't imagine driving for ten hours round-trip just to spend two minutes on my doorstep. It was very bizarre, and I have no idea how they found out where I live. I tried to be pleasant and get them back on their way as quickly as possible, but still let them know that I appreciated their support. The true comedy in this lies in the fact that I actually, in an effort to close my door behind me while I was standing on my porch, locked myself out of my house. In retrospect, that was funny.

Most people are looking for the same thing in life. I think we're looking to share things with someone who is like us, and with whom we can be ourselves. The ladies on my doorstep told me as much when they said, "You were so natural and comfortable with yourself on TV, and we just had to meet you!" Afterward I realized that their traveling there was a huge compliment in itself. And it made me feel good. Not that I'm inviting any other vans to roll up, mind you!

■

AFTER IT WAS announced that I was going to be the next bachelor, someone said to me, "There must be a lot of pressure on you, because you have to avoid a misstep at all costs." And this is true. I get nervous about screwing up on the show. Who knows? I might fall flat on my face. But now that I know I can pick myself back up, I don't worry so much about making mistakes.

I'm excited about doing the show, and I'm curious as to how it will all work out. I'm hoping that the women on the show will be more than just people who want to be on TV. I'm looking for a lot on the inside as well as the outside.

I'm going on the show to have the opportunity to pursue a relationship with someone who might be right for me, who I may never have met otherwise. Let's face it, we generally meet and marry someone who lives in or around the area where we live. I've lived in Michigan for more than thirty years, and I haven't met her. So why not go to California with an open heart and mind?

Lately people ask me what type of woman I'm attracted to. I have to say that I'm attracted to a lot of different types of women. I don't think I can pigeonhole what I like. Besides, a woman could be gorgeous by all accounts, but what's the point of being in a relationship with her if she has no personality, no sense of humor, no loyalty? The pretty face really isn't going to count for much. And anyway, as the old saying goes: Beauty fades, but the character remains. With that said, though, I definitely want to be attracted to her in every way.

■

THE TABLOIDS WERE horrible after the announcement that I was going to be the next bachelor. For example, one tabloid ran an article saying that ABC was scrambling to try to find women to go on the show, because no one wanted to be a part of it with me. In fact, the number of women who applied to *The Bachelor* was the largest of any they'd ever received. I think it might have been thousands of women applying for twenty-five slots. But here was this tabloid, inexplicably claiming that I wasn't attractive or wealthy enough to get any applicants.

By this time I was getting used to it, so I didn't really care if something negative was said about me. But then they started chasing after Jennifer, which was totally unacceptable. She didn't ask for any of this. I never thought they were going to find her, since her number is unlisted, but somehow they tracked her down. They've camped on her front lawn. It has just been a nightmare for her, and I didn't think that was at all fair. If I had known she was going to be harassed, I never would have agreed to be on the show in the first place.

When I learned that the paparazzi were after her, I called ABC and Telepictures and everyone I could think of to help me get these people to leave her alone. Jennifer knew I didn't want her to be bothered. She saw that I was doing everything in my power to protect her.

One surprising result of all this harassment by the paparazzi is that Jennifer and I have become a team once again. She knows that I'm going to bat for her—she can see it.

It's been an incredible turning point for us. We have had to get together to solve this issue, and when we did, we realized that we still love and care for each other and have a lot of respect for each other. The relationship will most likely never again be a romantic one, but I think we've finally reached the point where we can honestly be friends. In fact, Jennifer told me, "I can't believe I'm saying this . . . but I hope you find love." I was deeply touched.

At the time of this writing, the filming of *The Bachelor* is just days away from starting. Maybe doing the show is going to be a huge success—or a big disaster. I don't know. But I think the show will change my life for the better. I believe that as long as I'm honest with the women on the show, it'll be okay. Like everything else in my life in the past year or so, it's bound to be one hell of an adventure. I'm going into the show with the right intentions. After all, I've done all the things I've done over the past year or so with the right intentions, and everything *has* been going pretty well so far. And I'm tremendously grateful for the differences in my life that this past year has made.

I've realized that, for some strange reason, I've been given a second chance in my life. I've been given the opportunity to change the way I used to approach relationships and life, and a lot of the things that needed to be shaken up—and I was willing to do it! I've realized that every ounce of this experience up until now has been amazing. And I've loved every second of it.

I am grateful that during the worst time in my life I was handed an off-the-wall chance that changed everything. And I'm humbled that I've handled myself in a way that has inspired some people, made them identify with me, and made them laugh. That is the most wonderful thing of all.

Thank you for taking the time to be a part of this with me. As I write these words, I don't know what the outcome of the show will be. But by the time you read them, you will know, and so will I. Who knows? This past year has been so incredible. And I've realized that you can't control the future. Anything can happen. And in my life, it probably will.